Linthead

Linthead

Growing up in a
Carolina cotton mill village

Wilt Browning

Down Home Press • Asheboro, N.C.

ISBN 1-878086-00-6

Library of Congress
Catalog Card Number 90-083267

Printed in the United States of America

Cover design by Harry Blair
Book design by Elizabeth House

Down Home Press
P.O. Box 4126
Asheboro, N.C. 27204

To my children,
Ken, Vicky, Mark, Jenny and Andy,
and especially to my wife,
the mother who raised them.

Acknowledgments

There is a great emptiness deep inside that I was denied the privilege of placing a copy of this book in my father's strong hands. I must trust now that he would have liked what has been written here, because so much of it is his story.

And my mother's. They were patient when I came to ask questions, to pry at times. I could have written a book without their hands-on interest, depending totally upon my own fickle memory. But their memory of small details was so much clearer than mine that I could not have written *this* book without their help.

The encouragement and patience that came from my wife, Joyce, was an inspiration, as was the excitement of our children that their dad was writing a book that might actually see the light of print.

I owe a debt of gratitude, as well, to my fishing buddy Leland Hughes, who had the misfortune of growing up on a mill hill at Seneca, S.C., and not at Easley Mill. In sharing the memories of his own youth, Leland helped immeasurably in jogging my own memories. More importantly, like the football coach he is, he insisted upon results and helped me focus upon the goal of completing this work.

What is contained here, in large part, also comes

from the memory of two of the sports heroes of my youth, Paul Rampey and Juber Hairston. Both welcomed me into their homes for long taped talks about textile league baseball and other aspects of life on the mill hill.

I thank, too, all the people who helped with the collection of old pictures contained in these pages, because each one offered much more than fading snapshots. Each wanted to linger over family albums, sharing their own views of the life around the mill that each of us held so precious. So, I am indebted to J.B. Owens, my old midget football coach, who is back in Easley in retirement, still spending chunks of his time working with young athletes, and to Slick McGaha, who was a part of most of the mill baseball teams through the central part of the century. And to Harry Dalton's mother for letting me ramble through the keepsakes my friend left behind a long time ago, and to Troy McCoy, Earlene Townsend and Beulah Jane Galloway Holcombe.

The efforts of Ralph (Coon) Hendricks in providing photographic memories was essential, and from his interest and that of several others, including J.B. Owens and Slick McGaha, has come a resolve to hold an annual Easley Mill reunion.

And especially, I am indebted to Jerry Bledsoe, who encouraged me in this effort as well, and risked some of the financial resources of his company, Down Home Press, in the publishing of this first book.

Introduction

Mine was a sheltered childhood. I am sure of that now. For example, I was already a senior in high school when it happened.

"Where do you live?" a new acquaintance asked me.

"Over on Third Street at Easley Mill," I answered.

"You're a linthead," he said, a frown forming on his face as though he had just tasted something vile.

Yep. I'm a linthead, and proud of it. And therefore, you, my children, must be half lintheads, just as my maternal grandfather was said to have been one-fourth Indian. And I hope you will be proud, too.

You must understand that the label, new to me all those years ago, normally is not intended as a compliment, and was not offered that day with the same admiration one might find in other labels, such as "Oh, you're a genius." Or, "Gosh, you're handsome."

So, I hope this comes as no shock to you, my own children, to discover that I am a linthead.

My mother and father were lintheads. Two people who lived their lives and made their dreams out of the fabric of a cotton mill existence, and who, when they walked day after day along Third Street and finally climbed the gentle hill to the house at the end of the street, would seem more gray than they had been when they had walked away down that street earlier in the day. Lint, cotton lint, clung to their coal black hair, giving them the appearances of having returned from their labors wearing cheap theatrical wigs gone bad.

Lintheads. Proud people.

So, on the following pages, my children, you will read about lintheads I have known, many of whom I have loved. Real people, many now growing old with their memories, others long ago dead.

In remembering how they and I once were, I am compelled to be as honest as my memory permits from the distance of more than 30 years. In striving to hold my memory to the test of honesty, I, in no way, seek to denigrate the people who were born, lived their lives and died on the mill hills of the South. I would not, could not do that.

Mill hill people – lintheads – will understand that, for among all groups of people I have known, they are the most honest.

And, in all honesty, the times of which I write may seem to be difficult times, and I am certain they were for my mother and father in those post-Depression years when they relied on God, young love, pinto beans and cornbread to nourish them and their three children emotionally, physically and spiritually.

But hard times is not the product of any particular age. Hard times have visited your mother and me, and all five of you have come through your own tests, each finding triumph in your own ways.

So, feel no pity for these people of my memory. For yet another characteristic of most lintheads I have known is that they tolerate pity poorly. They are proud people, people with gentle hands and strong chins, people loyal to family, church and the cotton mill.

Lintheads, my children, and proud of it. Welcome to what was once my world, and that of my generation and those that came before us. For mine was the last generation to grow up and to leave the Southern mill hills of company-owned houses and semi-professional baseball teams and iron-wheeled wagons. Struggling now with the times and seeking their place in international markets, some of the mills are still humming away. Easley Mill, near which I grew up, finally yielded to market pressure and closed its doors for good as I was writing this book.

The houses are still there, and some of the people. But not the way of life that nourished me and my friends to adulthood. You cannot return today, as to a farm, and discover what it really was like, because this world no longer exists, except in the memories of us lintheads.

Those memories are offered here as an essayist might write them, for that really is what sports writers are. Especially sports columnists such as I. We are people who write in bits and pieces and who, according to my good friend and mentor, Irwin Smallwood, write upon the sand.

So, it is to this my sand that I go now so that you will understand that I too am a linthead, and proud of it.

Contents

A Death in the Family

At this very moment, it is 8:10 p.m., Friday, January 26, 1990. It has been a cold, partly cloudy day that has brought to a temporary end an unusually mild January.

In three hours and 50 minutes from now, Erwin Maddrey, a man I never knew, a latter day linthead, will turn out the lights at Easley Mill, close the big door behind him, lock it, walk to his waiting car in the empty parking lot and drive away.

After 89 years as one of the four major economic rocks of my hometown, Easley Mill will be dead. Tonight the last shift of workers will make their way home through the bitter night. They will never return.

There is a lump in my throat, an emptiness in the pit of my stomach, neither of which I can satisfactorily explain.

I left the mill hill and thus the mill when I was 18 years old and never came back except to bring one, and then another, of our infants home until they numbered five, home to get acquainted with their grandparents.

I did not at age 18, nor at any time since then,

plan to work in the mill, as had my mother and my father and his mother and father before him. My own mother, who first worked in the mill when she was fourteen years old, once misunderstood this resolve in me. She said that maybe I needed a few corners knocked off, that I considered myself too good to follow in the footsteps of my parents. Which, of course, was never the case. There simply was something about the smell of newsprint that I preferred over the smell of carded cotton.

Still, in a sense, she was right. Maybe it was something of a rejection. And as I think about that decision I made to leave home as a teenager, I realize now that it was more a generational decision than a personal one. And I hope my mother has come to understand that as well, though after all these years I still am not certain. In retrospect, I was part of a larger movement; almost none of my peers remained there. Mine was the generation that broke the chain.

Maybe we're part of the reason that on this night the old mill is dying. Maybe that I and others like me went away instead of remaining, as had generations before us, is part of the equation that added up in some cold corporate office somewhere to this closing. For whatever reason it is about to happen, this is a strangely sad moment for me, this very moment in which Easley Mill is running through its final shift. I didn't want this time to come.

It's like – how shall I put it – like something

permanent, irreversible. Like death. Yeah, that's it. It's like death. A death in the family. I don't know how else to explain what's happening in Easley tonight.

And now my memory is racing back to my own youth, to a time when the mill, and the community surrounding it, was alive, happy, vibrant, loyal. When my parents talked over weekend meals about the difficulty of the work, but were proud that Easley Mill turned out what was regarded by the industry as the best cotton broadcloth made anywhere.

So many people, salt-of-the-earth folks. Patriots to whom only God was more sacred than the flag. The mill hill is not suddenly a ghost town now that the heavy door is about to thunder closed for the last time. On this night, my own mother and father still live there at the end of Third Street, and probably will for as long as they live. And so will others.

I worry about what will become of those working there tonight who are too young to retire to the meager support of Social Security checks and even more meager mill pensions. What does a 50-year-old spinner or weaver do when there is no more spinning and weaving to be done?

There is not an overwhelming sense of relief on this night that I did not stay. Yet, I too would at this moment be facing this final chapter on my mill hill as a doffer or a worker in the card room had I remained. Where would a 52-year-old doffer find a market for the skills he had polished for more than 30 years?

I worry about the people I don't even know, the people keeping the sides running halfway through one last night.

But mostly, I wonder about the people I knew. Because this is their heritage slipping into the past. Where are all the names and faces I remember from the 1940s and 1950s? And where are all the names and faces who were there but who no longer register in my memory? And there must be many of those.

So many of them are dead now, most of their productive years spent in that four-story brick cotton mill on Fifth Street. And maybe that's best. Maybe this night would have broken their hearts.

So many of their names come back to me now, the names of the living and the dead who were there in those grand post-World War II years. And I wonder whatever happened to them.

Whatever happened to the Garrens who used to live down the street, or the Dunns? Whatever happened to the Waters family, whose house on Second Street burned to the ground one winter night, leaving the family with nothing but their lives? They didn't build the Waters house back; you don't rebuild mill houses. You just move on, and the Waters moved on.

Whatever happened to Aunt Nan Ledford, our neighbor across the back alley? She was probably somebody's aunt, but not the aunt of anyone with whom I was acquainted. Yet we never called her anything else. Aunt Nan was friendly, always smiling, caring for her mostly reclusive husband who also, I am told, had once been happy, friendly. But who came home from World War I carrying heavy emotional baggage, the victim of early chemical warfare.

And I remember her next-door neighbors, the Whites. In our youth, the mill hill was our paradise, but in his dying, Mr. White showed us that one person's paradise is another person's hell. He was found dead one morning in his car. Ant poisoning, they said.

And whatever happened to Squalie Merck, who lived at the corner of Second Street and Seventh Avenue, and who turned his back porch into a barber shop on Saturday afternoons, and who would give you the best trim on the mill hill for 25 cents?

The Sudduths. How many members of that family are left scattered, I would guess, about upstate South Carolina? Marvin, one of the sons closest to my age, died half a decade ago, when a tree he was felling for firewood to keep his home warm twisted and tumbled the wrong way. Marvin was crushed.

And the Cothrans, whose son Harold was older than I and whose other son Roger was younger. Harold and I, so caught up in a world war that we created of it our own games, dug foxholes in the pasture so deep that we once reached the white-sandy subsoil below the thick layer of red clay. Someone complained that the foxholes were dangerous for cows that may wander too close in, grazing on a dark night, but protested no more when another neighbor pointed out that no one on the mill hill kept cows any more. Where are the Cothrans now? And another of our peers, Harold Medlin, who lived next door to the Cothrans on Third Street. Never saw Harold cry, though our games of football were more brutal than they should have been. The harder we hit Harold, the harder he fell, the harder he laughed. Harold left home without really leaving home. Runs a successful automobile tire business not far from the old mill. Won't be getting many mill customers any more.

And the Owenses. What will keep Ray and Marion and Pug and Fred and Ben and all the others close to the home hearth now? And whatever happened to J.B., their uncle, once a grand athlete who was my first football coach? Funny. Every time I hear "I'm Looking Over a Four-Leaf Clover" on a Golden Oldies radio station, I think about J.B. because that's what was playing on his car radio the day he loaded his Buick with kids and set out to find and clear a YMCA camping site. Whatever happened to J.B.?

Hawk Waldrop, who lived on Fifth Street, and Harry Dalton, who lived on Eighth, are long dead. They were buddies of mine who would have found sadness in the day the mill closed, too. Hawk, so changed by disease I didn't recognize him the last time I saw him as he sat at the lunch counter at Joe's, where the world's best chilli-and-onion hamburgers are made, died a few years ago of cancer. Harry died a long time ago of a weak heart.

Oh, my! And the one who dodged death, Doyle Dyer. Older than I by a few years, Doyle was never a close friend of mine, but I knew him as a likable older boy who had become a teenager that day a shot rang out in a cluster of young teenagers who were admiring a handgun near the spring at the bottom of the hill in the pasture not far from our home, there where Easley's new post office will rise.

Doyle fell to the ground, the victim of an accidental shooting. The bullet struck him at the base of his neck, where the sternum and the shoulder blades come together to form that little dip below the Adam's apple. But from there, Doyle would tell me later, as he displayed the scars, the bullet miraculously traveled to the left and over his shoulder, finally stopping outside his shoulder blade.

As far as I know, Doyle also never worked in the cotton mill, but I think about him tonight, too.

I think of them all tonight, the Browns and Searcys and Putnams and the Galloways and the Newsomes and so many of the others. And I wonder whatever happened to all of them.

It was a long time ago that the mill sold the houses built of solid, substantial material, sold them more than three decades ago. Sold them for what, even in those low-inflation days of post-World War II, were bargain prices. So already the community had changed in a lot of ways. Now this. Now this final closing.

The silence along Fifth Street must be deafening tonight.

There must be a hundred reasons it has come to this. Maybe a good war would have saved Easley Mill, because as long as we were punctuating our history with intervals of armed conflict, cotton products seemed to be in great demand. But now peace has broken out all over and the mill has died.

I suppose that, in retrospect, we can place a lot of the blame on the government, because imports, especially those from textile plants in Japan, began taking a toll on the cotton mills of the South a long time ago. Long before the same sort of market intrusion was felt by the automobile, television, computer and a hundred other industries.

But now, on this night, when Erwin Maddrey will be the last worker out of the place forever, it doesn't matter what brought on this death. Only the dying, and the living that happened there for almost nine decades, matters now. Death for Easley Mill comes tonight, in the very month in which the old plant would have become 89 years old. Eighty-nine years, merely the blinking of an eye compared to the long run of the Industrial Revolution, of which the cotton manufacturing industry was a part.

Eighty-nine years. About what we, and apparently cotton mills, are promised on this Earth. Four score and nine.

I didn't fully realize it until this moment, but communities age, just like people. And maybe they, too, grow old and die. When I left my parents' four-room home for good at the age of 18, the mill hill was still a youthful place. There were children about, laughing and chatting and playing their way through the carefree years.

Now, in retrospect, I realize that every time I returned to that clean house that always has seemed like home, and to those wonderful meals in that perfect kitchen where we always bowed our heads and gave thanks for the gift of food, there were fewer and fewer children laughing and playing in the old neighborhood.

Now, also in retrospect, I realize that the neighborhood of my childhood was beginning to show its age. It was slowing down socially. It, as I, was turning gray around the temples.

Though a lot of the houses and some of the people, including my mother, remain there, living out their vigil, the mill hill of my youth dies tonight. At midnight.

And I am left with these ashes, these memories.

The author and his mother on the front porch, where long home runs landed. Photo taken around 1949.

The Super

The mood of that sunny summer day in 1946 had grown ugly and my father had gone inside, leaving me and my mother alone on the front porch of the house at the end of Third Street to worry about what would happen when the Newsomes and Mickey Hughes reached our front gate.

"What's going to happen?" I asked my mother, worried, almost whispering.

"I don't know. But don't worry about your dad. He's a brave man," she answered, though I was not convinced that she was herself without worry. She had stopped rocking back and forth in the big rocking chair, and she had stopped snapping and stringing fresh beans.

She watched the three men, young men, but men nonetheless, walk toward our house from the baseball field in the distance.

All this had started seemingly innocently enough. The war in Europe was winding down, and there was a widely held belief that if Hitler fell, Hirohito could not be far behind. And these Newsome boys and Mickey Hughes had done their part. Having been ripped from the last of their childhood years, they had been away at war and all had survived unscratched.

And now, on this perfect day, they were together again, playing simple games of roll-to-the-bat, trying to recapture, if only for a moment, that bit of childhood now lost to the years and to the confusing urges of young manhood.

When they had gone away, none possessed the power to send a well-struck baseball so deep that it could menace our family, whose house was situated not far from where the left-field foul line would have run had the field been extended that far. Which, of course, it had not been.

But now they were men, and they had the power, and when Mickey Hughes pulled an inside pitch, he tried to shout a warning to my mother who neither heard nor saw in time to shield herself and her beans.

The ball bounced once and crashed onto our porch not five feet from where she sat.

"I'm sorry, Mrs. Browning," Mickey called as I retrieved the ball and threw it back toward the sandlot baseball diamond. "Won't happen again."

But it did happen again. Only moments later, this time coming even closer to hitting my mother. And it might have had I not leaped to field the line drive cleanly before it could further threaten her. However, the ball had arrived at about the same time that my father stepped from the house.

"What's going on?" he asked.

"That's the second time they've hit a ball down

here," my mother said, just as I wound up to once again return the ball to the playing field.

"Give me the ball," my father said, just in time. And he carried it back to the playing field and stood for what seemed too long surrounded by the young soldiers back from the war.

"Don't do it again," I finally heard him saying in warning.

"And if we do?" someone pressed, challengingly.

"Just don't do it again." My dad's warning had a bite to it now.

Dad had just joined me and my mother on the front porch when yet another baseball, its flight announced by the unmistakable crack of the bat, flew in our direction.

"Don't touch it," my dad said to me.

The ball rolled to a stop against the root of the big oak tree.

"Throw the ball back, please," one of the men-children yelled from the distance.

"No," Dad said softly to me. There was tension in the air.

And now the men-children who had been off to war were marching toward our position and my father had gone into the house. He returned moments later, now wearing his working shoes.

"Are you going to give us the ball, or do we have to come take it?" one of the Newsome boys asked threateningly.

"I'll take care of the ball," my father said as he picked it up and placed it in his pocket.

"If the super wants to give it back to you, that's all right with me. But you'll have to talk to him about it this time," my father said. Then he walked through the yard gate, through the gathering at the street and disappeared down Third Street.

"Where's he going?" I whispered to my mother, suddenly proud, very proud, of my father for the bravery he had shown in walking through this cluster of handsome, now angry, young men outside our creaking gate.

"Gonna talk to the super, I guess," she said.

Taking a dispute to the superintendent of the cotton mill, the super as we came to know him, represented an appeal to the highest authority in our lives this side of church and God. And the trip my father was taking on this day, I would come to understand, was the perfect example of how power was structured in those days. For he walked within a half block of the Waldrop house, where our neighborhood's representative on the city police force lived, and carried his complaint to the executive offices at the mill three blocks away.

Mother later also would argue our case in the office of Mr. Underwood, the super. And when Mother asked to move to another mill house a long way from the baseball field, the super said that would not be necessary.

That, to my knowledge, the ball was never returned to the power hitters home from the war, and that we did not have to move, was proof enough for the rest of us that my father's and mother's case had been airtight. And, as far as I know, the Newsomes and Mickey Hughes never returned to that sliver of their childhood. Without question, they never again drove an inside pitch into our yard.

The power of the super, and thus the power of the cotton mill, over our mortal lives was considerable in those years. But already, much of the authority had given way, I would be told later in my life, to the changes that the 1950s would bring and that would be completed by the time that decade had drawn to a close.

Though my parents, for all the early years of their working lives, received their salaries in cash in small brown envelopes, there was a time in the lives of their parents – my grandparents – when the mills paid employees in script. Script that could be redeemed only in the company-owned stores in exchange for groceries, meats, feed for livestock and chickens, even for haircuts.

It was, I am told and have no reason to dispute, a life refreshingly free of major complications. All the company-owned houses were within easy walking distance of the droning cotton mill, so automobiles weren't necessary elements in our uncomplicated lives. And the mill provided shelter and, in a sense, clothing and food as well. And people took comfort in that.

Nobody called it "Big Brother" at the time, but that's what it was.

"Listen," Juber Hairston once said, and he

The Easley Church of God congregation, about 1952.

apparently had reason to know. "I'll tell you how much in charge the super was. If you got drunk and caused trouble on the weekend, Monday'd be moving day."

Yet, the mill and the super were not in charge of every facet of our lives. For the most part, decisions involving God and church were left to the individual.

Except for those tense months in the late 1940s when the labor unions, from which the textile companies had hoped to escape in their migration South from New England all those generations ago, arrived at Easley Mill seeking to organize. For long weeks, my father, who was soon to be promoted to loom fixer on the first shift, and my mother, who worked in the spinning room, talked quietly over Saturday and Sunday meals – the only ones they shared together with their growing family because of their varying work schedules – about efforts to organize, about the pressure they felt to resist.

It was a boom time for area churches. Sanctuaries that had long needed new pews suddenly got them, and the super was invited to Sunday meeting so that the donors, the faceless cotton mill executives in another city, could be properly thanked, and so that the new furniture could be dedicated.

Our own church had existed for years between a gravel parking lot and a dry cleaning establishment, and in the summer months when Sunday preaching dragged on into early afternoon and the heat of the day, the dust from the parking lot would swirl into the air and drift through the open windows. We arrived one Sunday to discover a fresh coating of black tar and gravel where the dust and dirt had once been. And there was a brand new piano to the right of the pulpit. They were gifts from Alice Manufacturing Co., the mill closest to the church, even though Alice was not involved in a labor election.

And we were thankful.

That was the Sunday that our preacher chose a particularly frightening passage as the text of his sermon.

"Let us turn to the Book of Revelations, the 14th chapter, verses 9 through 11," he said, then began to read aloud from the Bible opened before him:

> "And the third angel followed them, saying with a loud voice, If any man worship the beast and his image, and receive his mark in his forehead, or in his hand,
>
> "The same shall drink of the wine of the wrath of God, which is poured out without mixture into the cup of his indignation; and he shall be tormented with fire and brimstone in the presence of the holy angels, and in the presence of the Lamb:
>
> "And the smoke of their torment

> *ascendeth up for ever and ever; and*
> *they have no rest day nor night, who*
> *worship the beast and his image, and*
> *whosoever receiveth the mark of his*
> *name."*

"And, finally," our pastor said, "the 19th and 20th verses of the 19th chapter of the Book of Revelations:"

> *"And I saw the beast, and the*
> *kings of the earth, and their armies,*
> *gathered together to make war against*
> *him that sat on the horse, and against*
> *his army.*
>
> *"And the beast was taken, and*
> *with him the false prophet that*
> *wrought miracles before him, with*
> *which he deceived them that had*
> *received the mark of the beast, and*
> *them that worshipped his image.*
> *These both were cast alive into the*
> *lake of fire burning with brimstone."*

He closed the Bible so that the heavy sound of pages slapping together seemed to underscore the dreadful destruction foretold in these passages.

I was somewhat new to this, to this consideration of being tossed alive into a lake of fire and brimstone where, according to the words of Jesus in Mark's Gospel, there is a fire that never shall be quenched.

"Where the worm dieth not, and the fire is not quenched."

It was a passage of Scripture selected as the Biblical foundation for sermons in our church frequently. Why, I had suffered nightmares over the stories told from the pulpit of our church, stories of sinners screaming for mercy as they died, people who, still clinging to this life, could nevertheless already feel the flames of hell lapping at their feet, scorching, singeing.

I was not certain how my parents were affected by these messages of fire and brimstone. But for me, they were horrific images that burned into my young fertile imagination.

Such warnings of doom came as troubling intrusions. For much of my young life, I had been more concerned about whether a properly thrown curve ball should be gripped across or with the seams. And now this Sunday morning sermon made that seem frivolous.

It was a powerful sermon, a message perfect for the times, for the tensions my parents felt, for helping believers weigh the pros and cons of union membership as revealed by this servant of God and his interpretations of Holy Scriptures.

The conclusion to the sermon was shocking. The mark of the beast, the preacher said, would most certainly be conferred first upon union members, people who through greed sought more than their fair share from their employers. Though not only on union members, but on all of us who had not placed our trust in the Lord.

But certainly upon union members.

It was shocking to learn that there were, perhaps in this very church, perhaps in my very family, people who would vote for union representation and who, when that awful day arrives, would show up for work with a hideous mark upon their foreheads. Or in the palms of their hands.

I never knew, nor ever asked, if the same theme had been chosen as the sermon topic in other churches in our town and, particularly, in our neighborhood. It seems important now only in retrospect.

The devil's power being what it is, I wasn't certain it would happen. But the union lost the election by such a one-sided margin that organizers left town in humiliation. They never returned.

And for years after that, when we would see our super driving in his big car along Fifth Street, from the mill to the big, two-story white house set back amid aging oaks, we felt more fortunate than he that this was not a union town.

He had, we were sure, seen it as a money issue, as a challenge to the profit margin of the mill.

Some of us, on the other hand, knew it to be a far more serious matter than that. Mother and Dad, I was certain, and the rest had done the right thing to avoid The Tribulation and the mark of the beast. Some of our best friends could be lost to the beast, but that would be an individual decision. I found comfort for the moment, though, in the realization that we would not vote our way into the lake that burns forever with fire and brimstone.

A postscript to this memory would come much later in my life, in the very month in which the old mill on Fifth Street closed. My mother's boss had, during the days leading up to the union vote, asked my mother to serve as an informer for management.

What neither he nor I nor my father knew was that my mother, despite the fire and brimstone sermon that I remember so well, had determined to vote in favor of union representation.

"Certainly, I heard the sermon," she said more than 40 years later. "But I was and still am fully capable of thinking for myself and making my own decisions."

A proud linthead, my mother.

The Home Front

"Bringing in the sheaves...
"Bringing in the sheaves...
"We shall come rejoicing, bringing in the sheaves..."

My mother's voice was soft as she moved gently back and forth in the big rocking chair on the front porch. Reassuring. Comforting for a child as young as I was in those early years of World War II to hear my mother's soft voice in such a way.

In the far distance, so far away that the sounds of thunder could not be heard, streaks of lightning clawed at the gathering darkness.

"Mother, are we going to have a storm tonight?" I asked, interrupting her hymn.

"Not tonight. That cloud's too far away."

"How far, Mother?" I wanted to know. "Is it over there where the Germans are?"

"Not that far, but far away."

"Where the Japs are?"

"Oh, no. The Japs are even further away than the Germans. Are you worried about the Germans and the Japs?"

"A little."

Already, I knew a little about war, that somewhere, maybe there just beyond where the storm was raging on what seemed to me to be the edge of the world, my uncles, Jack, J.C. and Clarence. were fighting the Germans, and maybe the Japs. Because every night, as I prepared for bed, I was reminded to remember my uncles in my prayers.

". . .God bless Mother and Dad and Marlene and Doris and Jack and J.C. and Clarence and all the birdies and animals. . ." I knew that what my uncles were doing was worth praying for.

And there were the reminders that mine was not a peaceful world when I visited my grandmother's home, a four-room mill house a lot like ours with two Mothers' Victory Flags hanging in front-room windows. Each bore three stars, one for Jack, one for Clarence and one for J.C.

In my grandmother's living room was a big couch, and resting against each arm were colorful, silky, stuffed pillows adorned with military insignia and serpents and lightning bolts and the names of places a long way from home. Places like Monte Cassino and Omaha Beach. Places whose names I could not yet pronounce.

And on those special occasions when I spent the night at Mama's and Papa's, I could hear my grandmother praying deep into the night, praying that her two sons would be safe and that the war would soon end. They were soft, gentle prayers, barely audible over the sound of the Philco up-

Two photos of Jack Browning, the author's uncle, who served in the Army during World War II. These photos were taken at the author's house, probably in 1943.

right, the volume turned low, playing in the other room where my grandfather was listening to the nightly episodes of "Amos and Andy," "Fibber McGee and Molly" and "The Great Gildersleeve."

Papa left the praying to Mama.

Two strong people, each finding strength in the privacy of their own beliefs and their own thoughts, in their own ways.

They were special people who, it seemed to me, knew the reality of things even before they happened. Like that summer evening when a knock sounded at the front door.

"Sorry, Mrs. Browning," I could hear the stranger say, "but I have a telegram for you from the War Department."

She ripped it open and read rapidly, silently: REGRET TO INFORM YOU YOUR SON PFC JOSEPH F. BROWNING WAS WOUNDED IN ACTION. . ."

"Praise the Lord!" she called out. "Jack's not dead. He's wounded, but the Lord'll look after him."

And the Lord did.

Jack came marching home again, on furlough while the wound in his leg mended, giving him time to show off his new Plymouth four-door. And giving him time to become my hero.

"Wanna look?" he asked, handing me a small box. Carefully, I opened the lid. Inside was a beautiful thing made of ribbon and shiny medal, and shaped like a heart.

"It's my Purple Heart," Jack said, smiling. "They gave it to me when I got shot. Wanna see the bullet?"

"Sure," I said excitedly.

He reached into his pocket and drew out yet another small box. He opened it and there was a long sliver of medal, pointed on the end.

"That's it," he said. "The doc gave it to me when he took it out of my leg."

"Did it hurt?"

"Oh, a little."

"Did a German really shoot this bullet?" I asked, touching the cold metal carefully, as though it might explode, as though that very act would bring me closer to a real German.

"Sure did," my uncle said.

"I've never seen a German. But you have. Bet you've killed lots of them. I bet you're a hero. What happened to the one that shot you?"

"I don't know," he said. His voice had suddenly grown more somber.

"You going back, uncle Jack? You going back to fight some more Germans?"

"Yeah. Got to. Soon's I'm well enough."

"When will that be?" I was in no hurry to lose the first hero I had ever known.

"Not for a long time."

But Jack did go back, leaving me, my two sisters, my mother and dad and the rest of the relatives to do our part. Part of our part, I came to learn, was stillness itself, stillnesses known as blackouts when Dad would drape black cloths about the windows to keep light from escaping.

And each time the sirens in town wailed and the lights went out, I asked my father if the Germans were coming.

"Maybe not this time," he always answered. And I would listen to the sounds of the black night, listening for the sounds of German bombers. They never came.

Maybe the war was tough on our family, more difficult than I recall. For me, it was mostly a good time of playing marbles, and digging make-believe foxholes and shooting make-believe Germans. And occasionally, I would take an imaginary hit in the shoulder and reel under the blow. But gallantly I would fight back, ignoring the imagined pain and crouching lower in my shallow foxhole from where I fired yet more volleys at the imagined enemy there beyond the next terrace in the pasture next to our house.

My battles always ended conveniently, when Mother called me home to supper.

Mother and Dad had to deal with rationing which, I have read, was difficult. But, for us, for me, rationing seemed a small price to pay to help Jack, J.C. and Clarence fight a war for us.

Nylon was scarce, but I had little use for nylon in my young world. Gasoline was rationed, but we had no car. I knew of food-rationing stamps, but we always seemed to have enough, the five of us.

Born four and a half years before the attack on

Pearl Harbor, I was too young to realize that I and my sisters, who midway through the war came to number two with the arrival of Doris Ann, were the reasons my father wasn't marching across Europe with his brothers, Jack and J.C. Or battling in the South Pacific with Clarence.

"Dad," I asked more than once, "you won't have to leave us to go where Jack and J.C. and Clarence are, will you?"

"Maybe not," he reassured me again and again.

Month after month, the news from Clarence, Jack and J.C. remained hopeful. They were well, they wrote, and they thought about all of us a lot.

Jack even had been back home again ... sort of.

His furlough over and his leg healed, my hero was assigned to an Army post in Mississippi where his recuperation was completed.

He would be shipping out to Europe again in a few weeks, he wrote, and his company would be moved from Mississippi to a ship-out point in the Northeast. He would be coming through town on the troop train. And he would be looking for us at the crossing down near Glenwood Mill, on the right side of the track. If we could be there, he would try to wave to us. He guessed at the day and time and we marked it on our Liberty Life calendars.

Oh, we counted the days. Deep into the night, in the stillness of the sleeping hours, when trains would rumble through town a few blocks away, I could from time to time hear my grandmother

"Claude, you don't suppose, do you, that Jack's on that train and we got the day mixed up?"

"That's just an old freight train," Papa would assure her. And I wondered how he knew that.

Still, it would happen again and again as the days dragged by. "You don't suppose, do you..."

"No. It's three more days..."

"No. It's two more days..."

"Listen! Shhhhhh!" Mama said urgently, when the day finally came and the whole clan had assembled down by the railroad tracks at the mill crossing. "Do I hear a train coming?"

"I don't hear anything," my grandfather said.

"Well, listen harder then," she scolded him.

He seemed to be trying to listen harder. And finally, unmistakably, there was a rumbling in the distance.

"Here it comes!" Mama cried out, even before the train thundered into sight. "Now which side of the tracks we supposed to be on?"

"The right side, Mama," my father said firmly.

"Are you sure? What if Jack's on the left side of the train? Maybe we'd better split up, half of us over here, half of us over there. . ."

"But, Mama, if we do that, then only half us are going to get a chance to wave at Jack," my father pointed out.

Mama said something in response, but her voice now was being drowned by the wail of the train's whistle. As the big, smoking, coal-burning locomotive thundered closer, the whistle grew more urgent in its warning, as though the train-man was afraid that half of us may try to rush across the tracks at the last second just to make sure some of us got a chance to wave to Jack.

But we held our ground, on the right side of the tracks, there near the cotton mill. It was a frightful thing for a pre-schooler, feeling the earth trembling to the beat of the approaching power, seeing the steam, smoke and cinders flying from the stacks, being deafened by the endless whistle now.

Faces were pressed against the windows as the train thundered past. We searched the flying faces for one glimpse of Mama's son, Dad's brother, my hero.

"Here he comes!" my dad called out. Strange how he could do that, make his normally soft voice heard over deafening noise, a talent I came to learn that became one of the benefits of working a lifetime in the roar of a cotton mill.

In the distance, where one car ended and the next began, an arm dressed in army brown waved frantically. And the waving became even more frantic as the arm drew closer, close enough that we could see a sandy-haired soldier peering from the train, a big smile on his face.

"Smilin' Jack," I had heard neighbors call him, borrowing from the popular wartime comic strip by that name.

Then he was there, less than 20 feet from us, flashing by, still waving as the train rolled on into the distance.

For a long time, we stood there, the whole clan, without speaking, thinking how wonderful it had been just to see Jack again, to have been that close to him. And we watched the train grow smaller as it rumbled away. Long after it had disappeared beyond a distant bend, long after the sound of the locomotive had died away, we remained in the special place.

"Keep him safe, dear Lord," Mama said softly. And we climbed the hill, leaving behind the railroad and the crossing Jack had selected as our reunion place. "I'm glad we were all on the right side of the tracks," she said. "You saw him, didn't you, Wilton?"

"I saw him, Mama."

"I hope your dad never has to go away like that," she said.

"Dad, will you have to go away like Jack?" I asked yet again and again. "Will you have to go fight Germans?"

"Maybe not," he said.

But Dad finally ran out of maybe nots. "I've got to talk to you," he said to me that day in 1945. "You may have to be the man of the house for awhile."

"Dad, will you have to go away like Jack?"

"They're starting to draft people with children now, and I may have to go. Will you be strong if I have to go where Jack is?"

"I'll try," I said, my voice breaking, the tears starting to come. "When will you go?"

"I may not have to go at all. Alvoid and I will be

examined next week, and then they'll decide whether they need us or not."

The greetings for Dad and our next-door-neighbor Alvoid Galloway had arrived in the mail that day, delivered by our mailman, Mr. Nix, a cheerful sort whose daily rounds along Second, Third and Fourth Streets were announced by a chirping policeman's whistle which was his trademark.

Each time he climbed the steps to slip the day's mail into a waiting box, he accompanied the arrival with a couple of gentle blasts on his whistle, thus notifying the folks along his route that there were letters to be opened.

Or greetings from Uncle Sam.

But Mr. Nix delivered a lot of things other than greetings from the draft board. Like the sweet-smelling pink envelope he delivered to my father that summer, failing to note that the message was for another Browning who lived a few blocks away and who was working on his second marriage.

My father was waiting for Mr. Nix the next day and my mother lingered not far away when the chirping of the mailman's whistle grew closer to our house.

"This belongs to the other Browning," my father said, handing the unopened letter with the sweet smell back to the friendly postman.

"Oh, my," Mr. Nix said, getting a glimpse of my mother as he looked past Dad's shoulder. "I forgot that I'm not supposed to deliver that to you unless the missus ain't home."

The author's father, right, and
next-door-neighbor Alvoid
Galloway, in the mid-1940s.

And in the weeks to come, the whistling post-man would again and again remember the pink letter and the other woman it came to represent in his imagination.

"I hear the other woman's got a brand new electric washing machine," he said cheerily one day when Mother, who had been busy pushing heavy, wet clothes through a manual wringer, took a break and met Mr. Nix at the door.

Mother smiled.

"Hear tell the other woman's been wearing a brand new fur coat," he teased another time.

And yet another day, he asked, "Who was that pretty lady I saw Mr. Browning walking into Tinsley's Jewelry Store with the other day?"

"What'd she look like?" Mother asked, playing along.

And so the silly game went through most of a summer, until the day Mother reached for the day's mail when Mr. Nix climbed the steps to our door.

"They tell me, Mrs. Browning, that the other lady's been driving a Cadillac around town and . . ."

Mother began to weep. Her hands trembled as she held an unopened envelope in her hands. It was addressed to my father. The draft board had drawn his number and now Mother stood sobbing while our friendly postman tried awkwardly to end his playful conversation and to retreat down the steps leaving my mother alone with her sad-

the steps leaving my mother alone with her sadness and her uncertainty.

Mother met Dad at the back door the day he and Alvoid walked home from the bus station and their trip to Fort Jackson where they had undergone physical examinations and both had been found fit to join the war. Dad was carrying his induction papers in his hands as he climbed the steps to our back door, and Mother and Dad held each other close and talked quietly for a long time.

The War Department would be sending new Mothers' Victory Flags for the front windows of the house at Glenwood Mill, ones with four stars instead of three. Tears tumbled down Mother's face. She sobbed softly.

"You've gotta be the man of the house for a while," he finally said, rubbing the top of my head. I tried to be strong, brave, a man before my time.

The four of us – my younger sister Doris was still an infant – arose early that morning, the day Dad was scheduled to report for induction, before the sun had risen. My sister, Marlene, and I nodded without speaking when Dad told us to be good children and to take care of our mother and our new sister. Then he was gone, walking with Alvoid away down a back alley, not looking back.

We watched the two of them until they turned and disappeared along Seventh Avenue. Neither looked back. Their bus would be waiting in town, just a 30-minute walk away. And they would be gone. Dad would write, he had promised. And he

The tears burned our eyes and Mother hugged the two of us close for a long time. "Go back to bed and sleep for a while now," she said softly. "I'll get up and fix you some breakfast in a little while."

There was no sleep. The two of us, brother and sister sharing a room in a four-room mill house, lay in our beds not sleeping, not speaking for a long time. Marlene sobbed softly. I worked at being a man not yet nine years old.

"Dad'll be all right," I tried to assure my sister, trying to be brave, trying to be strong, trying to make my father proud of the man he had left behind.

The rosy dawn had just lost its rosiness and there was a gentle knock at the door.

Truth is, the three of us – my mother, my sister and I – may have been the first people on the mill hill to know that we were about to win the war. Dad's and Alvoid's personal war had lasted no longer than it had taken them to walk to town and back.

"They don't need us right now," he said as we rushed to greet him once again.

"What happened?" Mother asked between sobs of joy.

"There was a sailor at the door of the bus. He told us to all go home, that the war was just about over and that the War Department would get in touch with us if we were going to be needed."

"Dad, do you think you'll have to go where Jack is and fight the Germans?" I asked in a rush.

"Maybe not," he said as he hugged us to his chest yet again.

And for years we teased Dad that when the Germans and the Japs heard that he was about to join the war effort in uniform, they just lay down their arms and surrendered.

Juber and the Boys

The summer of 1954 was winding down and there was a hint of a chill on the night air as Fulton Roe and I sat in the bleachers at Dunean Mill watching a special Western Carolina Textile League baseball game, not aware that we were witnessing the end of an era.

Our team, the Easley Mill Rangers, had been trailing by three runs in the championship game when Hal Ensley came to bat with the bases loaded in the top of the ninth inning.

Hal Ensley, a rangy right-handed pitcher with a big kick, had been hired away a couple of years earlier from the Greenville Spinners, the Brooklyn Dodgers' farm team in the Sally League, then a Double A league just two levels below the majors at a time before free agency sent major league salaries soaring. Because getting rich in the major leagues then was rare and talent plentiful, it was possible in those days to hire good baseball players away from even the Dodgers, and Easley had lured Ensley away from his dream of making it some day to Ebbets Field. Lured away not to work in a spinning room, but lured away to play baseball, frankly, though the mills in those days legitimized the practice by putting good baseball players to work at soft jobs, which, in turn, caused resentment among mill workers for whom sports was not an important part of their lives. Ensley himself would some day work in the mill, though for a time during his playing prime he labored only as the recreation director in the big cotton warehouse near the mill that had, by the time Ensley arrived, been converted into a gymnasium. It was a convenient location for a gym because it adjoined the mill's bath house, a small building constructed to take care of the bathing needs of the community since almost none of the houses, even at that late date, had built-in baths. So, Ensley directed the basketball program and played baseball. As a pitcher, Hal Ensley had come with a bonus – he also was a hitter.

Even the nickname for the Greenville team, the Spinners, was a compliment to most of us lintheads. For it was a team that played its home games in Meadowbrook Park in a city filled with honest-to-goodness spinners, folks who labored in the spinning rooms of the dozens of textile mills that provided the economic base for the entire region.

So there the ex-Spinner Ensley stood in the batter's box in a textile league ball park not far from Meadowbrook, digging in, tapping his Louisville Slugger on the plate, ignoring the leather-lunged man sitting in the stands back of third base who was busy discussing Ensley's situation so that most of the fans, and especially Ensley, could hear some of the reasons he felt Ensley might have left the Spinners to play with this bunch of spinners and doffers and weavers from Easley Mill.

But Ensley blocked all that from his mind and concentrated on the pitcher on the mound 60 feet, six inches away, concentrated as the windup began, and concentrated as the ball spun toward him in the tantalizing spiral of a hanging curve. From the moment the crack of the bat had stunned the home crowd, there was no doubt that the old ball park would not hold this one. There were the telltale trots by the centerfielder and the rightfielder, half-hearted sprints in the direction of the ball that confirmed that Ensley's drive would not be caught. Ensley watched the ball with the rest of us until it disappeared over the fence and deep into the darkness to the right of the scoreboard.

Three runs scored ahead of him. Three runs that tied the game. And Ensley was well into his home run trot when he rounded third and headed to the plate where he would join his celebrating teammates already assembled.

In his jubilation, Ensley failed to touch home plate, an oversight that Fulton and I had not detected in our own jubilation, but one that didn't escape the attention of one of the Dunean players and the home plate umpire who, on appeal, ruled that Ensley was out at home. And, therefore, that

he had hit a three-run triple instead of a grand
slam homer.

So the score stood tied and for the moment, the
championship was still in doubt and the celebra-
tion would have to wait. And maybe never come.

It was a cruel thing, the sort of thing Ensley
would not have wanted to take with him into old
age. He had that to think about while Juber
Hairston, then a 44-year-old right-handed pitcher
with a herky-jerky motion who was playing out the
string on a long textile league career, held Dunean
scoreless in the bottom of the ninth.

Juber still was mopping his well-lined face
when Joe Anders homered on the first pitch in the
top of the 10th. This time, Anders made certain the
home run counted. Halfway between third and
home, his trot became a sprint and suddenly, in a
cloud of red dust, he was sliding home so that his
legs, his fanny and his back all were at one instant
or another squarely atop home plate.

Anders glared at the umpire as he confirmed
the obvious – safe at the plate.

Fulton and I were laughing about Anders and
his home run slide and about a championship for
Easley Mill as we found our way to my father's
1948 Chevrolet, with its vacuum shift gear assem-
bly, for our drive back along U.S. 123 to Easley.
Together, we replayed the final two innings pitch
for pitch until a flashing red light and the wail of
a siren got my attention. A highway patrolman,
now flashing his headlights, pulled in behind us.

I felt my heart thumping and felt my hands trembling on the steering wheel.

"Let me see your license," he said as he shined a bright flashlight into my face. Nervously, I reached for the metal South Carolina driving license clipped to my key ring.

"How long you been driving?" he asked.

"Three years," I answered, the shakiness of my voice confirming my nervousness.

"Long enough to know you were speeding," he said.

"Yessir," I said, though Fulton and I had been so engrossed in reliving the special game that I had not been aware that I had exceeded the 55 miles an hour limit.

"Where you live?" he asked, though my address was imprinted there on the metal license tag he now held in his hand.

"Third Street at Easley Mill," I answered dutifully.

"Whose boy are you?"

"Willie Lee and Martha Browning's."

"They know where you are?"

"Yessir."

"Where you been?" he pressed.

"To a baseball game at Dunean Mill in Greenville."

"Well, I'm going to do you a favor, son. I'm just going to write you a ticket and let you go. You can pay me or you can appear in court. Understand that?"

"Yessir." The highway patrolman began to write. Fulton and I sat silently for what seemed a long time and we were aware that passing cars seemed to be moving along more slowly than usual.

The highway patrolman handed me the ticket. "The fine's $18. You can pay me or the judge," he said.

"Dad's not going to like this," I said to Fulton when we were finally on our way.

"You got any money to pay the fine?" Fulton asked.

"Not a dime. Spent the last nickel I had to get into the ball park tonight."

We drove on, for the moment not speaking. In the trunk of the car, still in the big box in which it had arrived, was a new catcher's mitt, a big mitt guaranteed to be a popper, certain to make Hawk Waldrop's fastball seem even faster because of the noise it would create by merely crashing into the well-oiled pocket of that special glove.

"Fulton," I finally said. "You're going to be a catcher, aren't you?"

"Hope to," he said.

"Want to buy a mitt?"

"Not your new one. Not the popper," he said. Earlier in the day, before we had left home on our trip to Greenville and the playoff game, I had shown him my prized possession. I had pounded the pocket with my fist and Fulton had appreciated the special thud the special piece of leather was delivering as only those of us who dreamed could understand.

"Think about how Hawk's fastball's going to sound when it hits right there," I had said, driving my fist once again into the pocket, already thinking about next spring's high school baseball season.

I had handed the new glove to Fulton, and he too had pounded his fist into the pocket. "Wish I had one like that," he had said.

Now, he had his chance.

"Not your new mitt," he had said as we drove along, the joy of our evening now irretrievably spoiled.

"Yeah, the new one. Wanna buy it?"

"How much?"

"How about $18?"

"Your dad'll give you the $18," Fulton said. "And you know where that patrolman lives, up there on Old Greenville Highway. You can just take it to him and it'll all be over and you'll still have your glove. You don't want to sell that mitt."

"My dad'll give me more than the $18. He'll give me something else to remember. I'd just as soon he didn't know that I got stopped for speeding tonight. What about it?"

"Well, okay. I'll have to go into the house and get it when we get there. You sure $18's enough."

"Gotta be," I said.

I had planned to use that mitt come spring and the high school baseball season. But the dream I had not shared with my friend was my hope that I also would some day replace Carvin Medlock, the catcher on the Easley Mill team, and that would be the mitt, by then well broken in and enjoying a reputation all its own as the best popper in the league, that I would use when I finally took my place with Juber and the boys.

But that would never, could never happen. Fulton and I had watched an era come to an end at Easley Mill, and in a sense, on all the mill hills of the South that August evening in 1954.

Easley Mill withdrew from the Western Carolina League that winter, became a part of a county league for four more seasons, then finally disbanded its baseball team forever.

Television, with its snowy black and white pictures, was coming to the mill hills, and our habits were changing. The Saturday Game of the Week with Dizzy Dean and Pee Wee Reese and Saturday night wrestling seemed no threat to the life we had known. But it was.

Textile league baseball was dying before our eyes and we didn't know it.

Our old ball park, Underwood Field, is still there, but only as a sad reminder of what once was. Its lights that the mill hands, including my mother and dad, helped pay for by working an extra four hours on a Saturday many years ago have been taken down and mostly replaced by newer ones, the scoreboard that once stood just to the right of centerfield has disappeared and fire long ago ravaged the main grandstands. Though the old park has been reopened, all that remained for years was the weedy shape of a playing field and the tiers of concrete littered with broken glass and trash blown about by the wintery winds that have chilled our special place in the decades since the end came in 1958.

But, I'm telling you, children, there are ghosts where our old ball park once stood. Theirs are the names of special heroes, many of whom have died and others who have grown old waiting for a revival of mill hill baseball that will never come.

They are, among others, pitcher Juber Hairston, first baseman Charlie Gaffney, second baseman Joe Evans, shortstop James Campbell, third baseman John Connors, leftfielder Cotton Thomas, centerfielder Paul Rampey, rightfielder Guy Prater, and pitchers Roy Whitaker, Mike Nazinski and Paul Mason. The team of '51. Said to be the best team ever at Easley Mill since the team of '15 whose names are lost in the memories of dead men.

And there were others, people like Jesse Henson who failed to duck out of the way of an Earl Gray fastball one night at Brandon Mill. Bruised but not maimed, Jesse finished the season but played no more.

And there were so many more. They were the childhood heroes to a generation of boys who chased foul balls up Sixth Avenue and returned them in exchange for admission to the ball park.

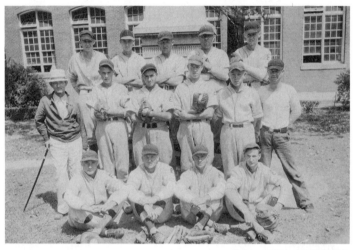

In 1936, this group of players won the Pickens
County Baseball League championships. Included
here are several who also played in the textile mill
leagues. Front row, l-r: Jim Spearman, Paul Merck,
Laurence McCall, Lloyd Cody. Second row, l-r: Jim
Smith (manager), Sam Spearman, Slick McGaha,
Red Owens, Ed Putman, Paul Mullinix (coach).
Back row, l-r: Ken McCoy, Lloyd Gillespie, Ed
Garrett, Fat Finley, Spurgeon Brown.

Hal Ensley, right and Joe Anders, left, were members of the 1954 Easley Mill team. Both players were hired away from the Greenville Spinners, a Class AA affiliate of the Brooklyn Dodgers.

And they were the heroes of the boys who knew where the breach in the left centerfield fence was and weren't too timid to use it.

They were the men who, frankly, made a lot of us feel superior. They were the best textile league baseball players in our town, though Glenwood Mill, Alice Mill and Arial Mill also fielded teams. Our team was better, played in a better league and that, therefore, was confirmation enough that ours was a classier mill hill.

Strange how funny that seems from the distance of all these years, a mill hill with a snobbish attitude. I'd never considered that until now. But that's what it was, the special gift these men gave to us, the last generation produced in the grand era of mill hill life in the South.

For them and for us, it is a memory grown sweeter by the year. Indeed, these baseball players are men who have grown old thinking about how grand it really was. They were men who still remember the big tree that stood in the outfield at Poe Mill because F. W. Poe, the man who owned the mill, refused to permit it to be cut down. And they are men who loved the old man for his love of that plagued tree, and the fact that every family on his mill hill got a large bag of fruit every Christmas for as long as he lived.

Poe loved baseball and the men who played the game.

Men like Paul Rampey and Juber Hairston whose real first name was William.

"Oh, I guess my dad gave me my nickname," he once said. "When we were sharecroppers down in Georgia and when I was just a baby, Daddy used to say this silly little poem:

" 'Juber this. Juber that. Juber killed a yaller cat.'

"And they just always called me Juber."

Actually, both Juber and Paul became our heroes by accident. Paul, once a minor leaguer in the Boston Braves organization, whose teammate on the way up through Salisbury, N.C., in the Piedmont League, Evansville, Ind., in the Three I League, and Hartford, Conn., in the Eastern League had been the great left-handed pitcher Warren Spahn, had found a home at Slater Mill when he decided he would prefer to retire from pro baseball than to be bought by the Chicago White Sox.

The Fourth of July always was special for Paul, and when he asked for the week off in 1941, his boss at Slater Mill turned him down. When Paul took the week off anyway, he was fired and wound up at Easley Mill where some of his relatives worked and where his darting, dark eyes and his famous smile and his special flare for the game would give our team a special personality for most of the 1940s and 1950s.

Juber, on the other hand, came to the mill hill as part of the migration from the cotton fields of the South that took place in the 1920s and '30s.

He was the eighth of 11 children born to share-croppers living three miles from Royston, Ga., not far from the home of baseball Hall of Famer Ty Cobb. In all the years the Hairstons had planted, nurtured and harvested cotton on the red-clay land of north Georgia, there had been only one good year. In 1918, the Hairstons averaged almost a bale a day when cotton was selling for $3 a hundred pounds. And for a time, the family could bring in as much as $15 a day.

They were good times, so good that Juber's mother made a trip to town and purchased one new outfit for each of her 11 children, and one new pair of shoes for each.

But in the dark of an early winter night, fire broke out in the small wood frame house where the Hairston family lived and only one of Juber's brothers had time to rescue his new clothes. He hung them on the clothesline while he tried to help rescue other family belongings and returned to discover that his new clothes, ignited by a spark, also had been destroyed.

For three years more, the Hairstons stayed on the land. If the fire of '18 had been devastating, the infestations of boll weevils in '19, '20 and '22 were even more humbling. And by harvest time, 1922, the Hairstons had taken flight and had sought a new life scattered among the mill villages of north Georgia and South Carolina.

Thus, Juber had come to be one of us.

Over the final two decades of textile league baseball in the South, the Ensleys and the Anders would come and go, but there would be until the end a Rampey and a Hairston on the team. Neither, of course, had been there when mill workers began to organize competitive baseball teams. But both began in the 1930s when there was no holiday more grand in the South than the Fourth of July.

"In those days, you'd play a doubleheader beginning at about 10 in the morning on the Fourth at Liberty Mill and everybody'd bring a big basket of food and you'd have dinner on the grounds," Juber said. "Then you'd drive to the other town and play the second game of the doubleheader there.

"Unless you were playing Pelzer. Then you'd play both games at Pelzer because they'd have dinner and harness races between games and it was something special."

The last of the Fourth of July doubleheaders was played in 1942. Beginning in 1943, the mills started shutting down for vacation for the week of the Fourth, and another tradition came to an end.

Juber pitched until he was in his late 40s, but never better than in that league championship series against Dunean in 1954. In the final three games, Juber had pitched five innings in relief on Tuesday, had worked 13 innings as the starter on Friday night, and relieved Ensley and finished the final seven innings of the game and got the victory in the Saturday extra-inning game that determined the championship.

"Know those packages of Anacin tablets you used to get 12 to a pack?" he asked years later. "My arm was hurting so bad those last two games, I took 11 Anacin tablets both nights just so I could keep pitching."

Juber survived and pitched for four more seasons in the Pickens County League. And he was there when the end of the era came once and for all and is a footnote to that moment in our history.

"The fall of '58," he said, speaking softly, sadly. "I pitched the game. Lost to Pelzer at Pelzer, 3-0. When they put up the bats that night, they never got them out again for a mill team.

"It was all over."

It had been an especially lucrative era for Rampey and Hairston and a lot of the stars who played through most of three decades, and who in the 1930s rode to road games in the bed of a mill truck equipped with solid rubber tires and a steam whistle, a bumpy old truck driven by Cash Williams whose son, Cash Jr., would become the sheriff of Greenville County.

Both Rampey and Hairston played in the primes of their careers for more than one mill team at a time. And that was not unusual.

"I played 21 years for Easley Mill," Hairston said. But in 1943, he also played for Mills Mill, for Poinsett Mill in '44, Laurens in '45 and Clinton in '48.

Indeed, in 1947, he and Rampey played as teammates at Easley Mill, then occasionally wound up playing against each other, Hairston for Laurens and Rampey for Joanna Mill.

Slick McGaha, left in upper photo with Edward Putnam in 1936, had a long career with the Easley Mill squad. Below, McGaha is shown at far right of front row, a member of the Easley team from the 1955-57 era.

Photo courtesy of Slick McGaha

Photo courtesy of Slick McGaha

"I was a pitcher in Easley and a catcher in Clinton," said Hairston who, by 1948, was earning $64 a week for his 48-hour job in the mill, but who was getting $100 a night as a catcher for the Clinton team.

They later would also face each other when Juber signed on at Laurens and Rampey at Monaghan.

"I played with some great ones," Juber said years after it had ended. "But Ramp was the best I ever saw. Made the best catch I ever saw, too.

"We were playing Arial Mill in a playoff game over at Meadowbrook Park one night. Harold Dunn was pitching and Paul was playing centerfield, and we had a 5-3 lead in the bottom of the ninth. And Arial had two on and two out.

"The batter for Arial hit a long drive over the leftfielder's head. The leftfielder gave up on it, but Paul made a back-handed catch just as he hit the tin wall in the outfield. He was so fast.

"And he was a great hitter. I remember one night at Underwood Park, we were down by two runs in the bottom of the ninth and Ramp and I were coming to bat back-to-back in the inning. We were sitting together there in the dugout and Ramp turned to me.

" 'Jube, the only way we're going to win this game, you know, is if both of us hit home runs and get us into extra innings.'

"That Joree went up there and hit one out in right center and I followed with a home run in left center. Then he got walked in the 11th inning and I followed with a hit. He scored all the way from first base on that thing."

Indeed, Rampey, along with big George Blackwell, who played himself into a legend at Southern Bleachery and Taylors, was one of textile baseball's leading home run hitters. In his 70s, Rampey was unable to even guess how many homers he hit in his more than 20 years at Easley Mill.

"Used to be, when you'd hit a home run," he said, "they'd give you things like a free haircut or a lube job for your car. One year, they also gave you a crate of soft drinks for every homer.

"I remember my brother Perry and I took our families to the mountains for the Fourth of July vacation that year and we took 37 crates of soft drinks with us." Most had been won by Paul.

It also was an era in which fans in the stands displayed their appreciation for big hits or well-pitched games by passing the hat.

"That happened a lot," Rampey said with that still familiar smile of his. "First time it happened, I got $11.25. At that time, when I worked a full week in the mill, I got $9.25."

"Most I ever saw was a hat full of money when Red Rogers passed the hat after the best textile league game I ever saw," Juber said.

"Happened in 1943 when we played Monaghan. Lou Brissie pitched for Monaghan and Wayne Johnson pitched for Easley. Both were home on leave from the service and both were pro players."

Indeed, Brissie, a big left-hander with an outstanding fastball, would pitch for the Philadelphia A's until severe war injuries to his right leg cut short a promising major league career.

"Never saw a game like it," Juber said. "There were no walks and no errors and Brissie and Johnson struck out 40 batters that night. Brissie got 22 of us, and Johnson got 18 of them.

"But we – well, not me because Brissie struck me out four times that night – got six hits and beat Brissie and Monaghan Mill, 2-0.

"Best game I ever saw."

Best game Rogers, an Easley pharmacist, ever saw, too. When he had passed the hat and counted the money, he had collected enough to send Johnson home on a plane to visit his relatives in Kansas before reporting back to his military company for deployment to Europe.

It was a league filled with talent and characters and Juber was at home in both categories. So was George Blackwell, who was built like Babe Ruth, who had a lot of power, and who, despite his size, was one of the fastest players in textile ball in his time.

"But he'd spit on his glove and he'd spit on his bat and he'd spit on you if you didn't watch him," Rampey said.

"Ol' George," Juber said. "I remember the night I got two strikes on him and decided I'd just slip the fastball past him and strike him out. He hit the thing out of the park.

"Next inning, I came up and George was pitching. I had a piece of mill cloth in my back pocket and I pulled it out and wiped my face with it. It was really hot that night. Ole George saw me and yelled at me.

" 'What's the matter, Juber? Got the blind staggers?' " It was a not-so-subtle reference to Juber's drinking habits in the days before he got religion.

"Then he tried to throw a fastball past me, and I hit it out of the park. He chased me and cussed at me all the way around the bases."

How good was textile league baseball in its peak years?

"Look," the old pitcher said, "I'm satisfied we could have beaten the Greenville Spinners seven out of 10 games and I'm satisfied we could have beaten any minor league team this side of Triple A in a short series. No doubt about it. Because we had hired away some of their best players.

"We had a left-handed pitcher, one of the best I ever saw, named Roy Whitaker. Got him from Asheville in the Sally League. Our manager was Joe Anders who played third base and the outfield for us. He'd played third base for the Spinners.

"Freddie Marsh was the best right-handed power hitter I ever saw. He signed with Cleveland for $6,000 and George Kell beat him out for the batting title in the International League by one point.

"And there was Ensley from the Spinners and

The Glenwood Mill baseball team, around 1915. Front row, l-r: Joe Edens, Guy Tanner, L.P. Fortner, Charlie "Shot" Reese. Back row, l-r: J.J. Sims, Monroe Pridmore, Clafe Rice, Maynard Spearman, Jess Stone, Erv Loftis, John Taylor, Matt Spearman.

Photo courtesy of Ralph Hendrix

Juber Hairston and Paul Rampey were two mill league stars. In 1954, Rampey, right, poses at the ballpark. In 1956, Hairston, shown in top photo in back row at far left, coached this group to the Pickens County Baseball League title.

Photo courtesy of Ralph Hendrix

Johnny Gray who signed with Detroit for $10,000.

"One of our pitchers in 1952 was Tom Sturdivant who was winning 16 games for the Yankees two years later. He got the most money I know of anybody getting. He was in the service stationed down at Shaw Air Force Base at Sumter. And he'd drive back and forth when we had a game and he'd get $250 a game.

"I don't recall anybody ever scoring off Tom. And he could hit, too. I remember he won one game, 1-0, with a base hit in the 10th inning."

In earlier seasons, it also was a league in which Shoeless Joe Jackson played out his exile from the big leagues as the key figure in the Black Sox scandals of 1919. Jackson was a linthead like the rest of us, born and raised at Brandon Mill near Greenville, the mill and the team to which he returned when he was kicked out of the big leagues.

Jackson also managed for years at Monaghan and Brandon and rewarded outstanding performances by his players with fifths of whiskey from his West Greenville liquor store. He also strolled around town with his famous bat, Black Beauty, in his hand and probably went to bat for the last time at the age of 53. A pinch-hitter, Jackson tripled off the base of the centerfield fence at Brandon and apparently never played again.

Shoeless Joe, Brissey and a few others are the exceptions. Textile league baseball included a roll call of heroes and characters mostly forgotten now. Folks like the speedy Lonnie Holder and Earl

Wooten at Pelzer, and Mack Bannister who was maybe the best of the umpires, but who called balls and strikes from behind the pitcher's mound. And there was the legendary left-handed pitcher Earl Gray of Dunean and Brandon, and Glenwood pitcher Squiddy Galloway, who lined his belt with tacks and with them he would scratch grooves into the baseball to make his curve even more frightening. And Easley pitcher John Smith, a left-hander who was famous just because he had a mustache and wore his wrist watch in the game.

It was a brand of baseball remembered almost as much for the characters in the stands as for those on the field, for fans like Stormy Bolen, who used to climb onto the chicken wire backstop behind home plate to torment the umpire, always with the same insult:

"I'm not going to call you what you are!" he'd yell. "But I hope when you go home, your mama comes running out from under the floor and bites you. You hear me, Mr. Umpire?"

We all heard.

And a lot of us remember.

The Kingsmen Quartet, one of the favorite's of the
author, who was blessed with an "uncertain tenor."

Born to Sing Bass

And so it was that my chance to become Easley Mill's next Carvin Medlock passed. Ah, had I been born only five years earlier. But in the late 1950s, Underwood Field would become nothing more than a good sandlot baseball park. And in another decade even that reminder of the old ball field's former glory would fade as well. Our mill hill, our neighborhood was changing.

Strange how in the final years of the 1950s the mill hill, now without its boys of spring and summer, seemed to grow old, even in its people. There no longer seemed to be the renewing of the generations, the steady march of sons and daughters to the mills, as though there were a sacredness to that tradition.

In the late 1950s, the children seemed to begin to disappear from the streets and the few remaining cows left in the pasture where we once played baseball reclaimed the diamond of our dreams. And there, the grass, the bitterweed and the thistles grew and prospered.

They finally even shut down West End Ele-

mentary School which had served our neighborhood for years. It was there that most of us first
learned that there were people who grew up on
farms, and who were so unfortunate as to have
never met Paul Rampey.

It's true. The village was aging. The graying
of America must have begun on the mill hills. And
now in those sturdily built homes, the last generation to rent company-owned houses is living out a
retirement softened only slightly by modest cotton
mill pensions. Once busy, once active, the mill hill
is today a mostly quiet place. Today, the cry of a
baby and the chatter of the few children left seems
to be an intrusion upon the tranquility of the place.

The mill itself has died, barely making it into
the final decade of the century. As industry and
industrial revolutions go, mill hill life was no more
than a flicker, lasting, in the case of Easley Mill,
just 89 years.

Of course, none of us in the late 1950s and early
'60s was wise enough to see it coming, to appreciate what was happening to the life we, the last
generation to grow up on the mill hill, had known,
as had our parents before us and their parents
before them.

People who write history seem always to be
finding turning points, slivers of time when corners were turned, when nothing would ever again
be the same.

With the perspective of an aging linthead, I
know precisely when the lives of our family changed

and when mill hill life as we had known it made a sharp turn toward the future.

As is so often the case, it happened in the name of progress.

Maybe we Brownings living at the end of Third Street were among those families who would be modern pioneers. Ours had been the second house in our village to have a built-in bathtub. The Arthur Winchesters, with whom my mother and dad once had shared a mill duplex, were the first.

We also were among the first in our neighborhood to push the old upright Philco radio into the corner to make room for television. Aunt Nan Ledford, our neighbor across the back alley, who was an aunt to none of us but carried the honorary kinship as a special badge of affection, had the first television set of which I was aware and she regularly invited me to watch the Friday night fights at her house.

It was only a matter of time, I knew, until my father would yield to the pressure. There was that religious question to be considered: Was watching television like going to the movies? And if so, was it a sin? The annual Rose parade on New Year's day, even in the years long before color pictures, would help resolve that moral dilemma. God had created the flowers and, maybe, had given us television so that we could see what marvelous parade floats could be created from his special gifts.

And when that first television set arrived at

our house, it was a grand thing, that black-and-white RCA that became the center of attention in our living room. I needed it, I felt, to feed my appetite for baseball now that the mill was curtailing its sponsorship of the community team. That and the Tournament of Roses parade had been the case I had presented to my father in trying to persuade him to buy a TV. And there was some justification. Dizzy Dean and Pee Wee Reese already were well-established as the experts on the Game of the Week. That the Saturday Game of the Week was sponsored by a beer, Falstaf, was but a minor hurdle to be overcome in our sober household. Before our first season of televised baseball had come to an end, I could even imitate Falstaf's Old Professor better than anyone on our street.

And Saturday by Saturday, Carvin Medlock lost his place as my baseball hero, giving way to Stan Musial, Gil Hodges and Duke Snider.

Perhaps the end of textile league baseball would have been more traumatic for me had it not been for that wonderful RCA. And perhaps we would not have been able to buy that television that I had so much admired at T.E. Jones & Sons Furniture had I not arranged the first business deal of my life.

I had told my father how much our lives would be enriched if we had a TV set, though I am sure I didn't state my case in exactly that manner. "Maybe some day," he had answered again and again.

Dad was good at that. He seldom said "No."

"Maybe some day" was better. It was no promise, though we took it as at least a ray of hope. In his wisdom, Dad kept us hoping. And reaching.

But in the matter of our first television set, there was a new element involved in my efforts to win my father's approval. For the first time in my life, I too was a man of means. I arose at four every morning and delivered the Greenville News to 105 of our neighbors, and every Friday and Saturday I made the rounds collecting the weekly subscription fee of 35 cents.

I would save my earnings, I suggested to my father, and I would be responsible for the payments on a new television every other month. It was a deal too good to turn down, and my father and I carefully, tenderly carried that new RCA up the short flight of stairs to our front porch and then into the living room.

The thing changed our lives.

In an important way, it also enriched our lives, especially mine.

For years, our radio on Sunday morning had been tuned to WESC, 660 in Dixie, or to WFBC, so that we could listen to the Palmetto State Quartet, the Kingsmen and other gospel singers as we waited our turn in the bathroom and dressed for Sunday School and preaching.

Already, I had accepted the possibility that perhaps my future lay not back of the plate as Carvin Medlock's replacement as the Easley catcher, but that it might be nice to sing bass for the Palmetto State Quartet. That I neither had a bass voice nor was likely to have one was never a serious consideration. With that television tuned to baseball or to gospel singing, I could dream any dream I wanted.

In living black and white, now we could watch a long parade of gospel quartets on Sunday morning.

And I came to memorize the bass parts for all the best gospel songs of the day. I particularly liked the booming "Oh, my lordy, I pray" part in the song, "There Will Be Peace In The Valley For Me."

If I were not going to be a baseball catcher, I must have been born to sing bass, I decided, though I noticed that I had been dealt an uncertain tenor voice, a misfortune that did not discourage me. As a catcher, I had not been blessed with a particularly strong throwing arm either.

Indeed, I had been encouraged in such bassy dreams.

Perhaps the best gospel pianist I have ever heard, Junior Cape, played at our church on Sunday mornings, Sunday evenings, Wednesday evenings and Saturday evenings and every evening of every revival we ever had. And we had lots of them. Junior, as was the case with most of the adults I knew, worked in the cotton mill. He played the piano only as an avocation. So wonderful was his work on the keyboard, he always seemed to me to be miscast as a second-shift spinner.

But we were lucky to have him as part of our congregation and knew it. Indeed, it almost was worth it to sit through all the fire and brimstone sermons of my youth just to hear Junior play the piano. We also were fortunate to have among our faithful the Roach Trio – Amanda, Cora and Calvin – two sisters and a brother who sang at the church on West Main Street in Easley for decades.

Cora played the piano for the threesome – not as well as Junior Cape, but well – and Amanda and Calvin stood near her and the three sang so sweetly that old-time members often cried. And occasionally, their singing would so move the spirit within us that we would begin clapping our hands in time to the music, and the singing went on and on.

To this day, I still wish every Easter that the Roach Trio could sing once again, just for me, the song they sang in our church every Easter of my childhood.

"On a lonely road was walking
two disciples gently talking,
and a stranger overtook them on their way.
It was Jesus who was risen
and their sins had been forgiven
and their hearts did leap within them on that day.

"Yes, He's risen here today.
He's no longer where He lay.
He is risen for I feel Him in my soul..."

In a sense, Calvin Roach and Paul Rampey had a lot in common as far as I was concerned. Paul had played pro baseball for a time in the Boston Braves system as a minor league teammate of Warren Spahn, who was on the way to a Hall of Fame major league career. Calvin, on the other hand, had been called to fill in from time to time as the lead singer for the Palmetto State and several other quartets, and, in my mind, there could be no greater accomplishment.

In baseball lingo, it could be said that Calvin had a cup of coffee with the Palmetto Staters. And I was impressed. That was all the confirmation I needed that if he were not a great gospel singer, he was almost a great one.

And so it was to that sort of wonderful music that I was exposed for much of my young life. To this day, some of the warmest memories of my youth have to do with gospel singing.

Like the time the Kingsmen Quartet came to our church for a Sunday night singing and parked their big bus near the front of our small parking lot so that passersby knew something special was taking place inside. I remember that I sat entranced through the whole evening. And while I no longer remember anything they sang – though almost certainly they did "There Will Be Peace In The Valley For Me" – I remember that their bass singer was named Steamboat.

Steamboat showed off that night. I remember that, and I remember being impressed and wishing that Sunday night service would never end.

But it did. And now, we had the RCA plugged

in there in the living room, and every Sunday morning there were the Palmetto State Quartet, The Kingsmen, the Statesmen and the Oak Ridge Boys in the era before they hit the big time as something other than gospel singers. Like the mill hills of my youth, the Oak Ridge Boys changed more than I wanted them to in the years that were to come.

For a while I sang along with them on Sunday mornings. There even was the Palmetto State Women's Quartet. It wasn't the same. They had a bass singer, but to my ear, she was no Steamboat.

So, now I had at the flick of a dial the best of my dream worlds, baseball and gospel singing. But our family was being introduced to a lot of new worlds on television. I no longer tuned into the Monday night radio broadcasts of the Cities Service Band of America and my mother and father no longer listened as frequently to *The Great Gildersleeve* and *Amos and Andy* on the old Philco. Instead, we became regular watchers of I *Married Joan* and *Father Knows Best.*

WFBC-TV, channel 4 in Greenville, became our favorite channel and Monte DuPuy and Stowe Hoyle, the Texaco weatherman, became so familiar to us that we spoke of them on a first name basis. Though I already had left the mill hill and married by then, it was the summer I was to enlist in the Air Force that I finally accepted the truth I had for so long denied, that Stowe Hoyle also was Mr. Howdy Doody on the afternoon kid's show.

Ah, the pain of growing up.

If ours was among the first families in our neighborhood to purchase a television, we perhaps also were among the first to adopt new heroes. The new Wednesday Night Fights were not a hit in our house because Wednesdays were Prayer Meeting nights.

But we hurried home from Young Peoples' Endeavor on Saturday nights at church to watch professional wrestling, and a young newcomer named Ricky Star, who wore fancy shoes adorned with stars, became my favorite. My dad's tastes ran more to the stylish, dependable work of old-timer Lou Thesz. And together, the two of us sat transfixed on Saturday evenings, pulling for the good guys, hating it, feeling somehow cheated when the villains won even a fall. There were times when it seemed we were the only people in the world who had seen the bad guy slip a jagged bottle cap beneath the waistband of his shorts in some diabolical scheme to hurt a good guy. Even in black and white, the sight of blood seemed so real, so frightening.

So affected by pro wrestling were we that it was only a matter of time before we'd be there to cheer for our favorites in person. WFBC taped wrestling shows in its studios in Greenville each week and we wrote away for tickets.

The day they arrived, it was as though we had received tickets to the World Series. I counted the days.

I felt nervous when my father and I, arriving early for the wrestling show, climbed into the bleachers so that ours would be the best vantage points in the house.

The lights were bright, the ring large, and the crowd would become noisy by the time the two wrestlers who would battle in the first match, a one-fall, 15-minute time limit affair, strutted into sight from a distant door.

Dad and I cheered the good guy, who seemed to be waving to me as he strutted around the ring, awaiting introductions and the bell.

Dad and I still were strongly voicing our support as the match began. And the whole room seemed to bounce with the thundering report of every body slam. Almost at the same time, my father and I grew silent. We strained to watch closely.

"Dad," I whispered. "He really didn't hit him. Just made it look like it."

"I know," he said.

Everything had seemed so real, so violent on television. Live wrestling wasn't the same.

We left early that night and drove back along U.S. 123 to Easley mostly in silence. Perhaps my father had known all along that these were snake oil salesmen in their briefs. But I felt betrayed, more worldly, more wise, more grown up that night. Maybe that's why my father had taken me to the live show. Maybe he knew it was time for me to start growing up.

And maybe he was as disillusioned as I.

We became Lawrence Welk fans, and Ed Sullivan and the "Colgate Comedy Hour" now had more appeal to us than "Saturday Night Wrestling." But we still had the gospel quartets on Sunday morning, though they, too, were changing.

Everything about us was changing. We were growing up and the mill hill was beginning to grow old. Yet, to this day, on those rare occasions when I spin across the stereo radio dial in my car and happen upon a gospel quartet, a chill runs down my neck and once more I think how wonderful it would be to hear the Palmetto State Quartet singing just once more an old foot-stomper, heavy on the bass. Something like "Lead Me To That Rock That Is Higher Than I."

Or the Roach Trio on an Easter Sunday singing once again "He Is Risen Here Today."

"On a lonely road was walking
two disciples gently talking
when a stranger overtook them on their way..."

Noise in Paradise

Not many of us who grew up on the mill hill understood that we lived on the lower end of the economic scale until we were closing in on adulthood. We were too busy enjoying growing up in our paradise to understand that there were those, even in our own elementary school, so unfortunate that their fathers knew nothing about building wagons that rolled on iron wheels.

Because, truth is, if you have never thundered down a mill village street at the controls of an iron-wheeled wagon, you've missed something. So thrilling is that experience that more than once in the years when my own sons were growing up I considered taking hammer and nails in hand and building such a wonderful creation for them to enjoy.

I resisted. They would not have understood. Nor would our neighbors.

There are today no iron-wheeled wagons of which I am aware. There are museums that have dedicated their missions to preserving the American heritage. Yet none, as far as I know, has an iron-wheeled wagon to collect dust and memories.

It is one of the things of which I am most proud, most thankful – that mine was the last and probably the most enthusiastic generation of iron-wheeled wagon lovers.

And I know that I am fortunate to have been the perfect age when Mac and Cora Lee McCrickard moved next door to our house near the end of Third Street.

I was lying on my bed in the room I shared with the older of my two sisters the day the McCrickards arrived. I peeked through the clean, lacy curtains of my open window when I heard a car enter the driveway next door and stop.

The four-room house, a duplicate of our own home, had stood empty for several months while it was being renovated, its hardwood floors sanded and freshly varnished, its sandy-plastered interior walls freshly painted, the scattering of used automobile parts left behind by Alvoid and Ina Galloway loaded into the back of an old pickup truck and hauled away.

And now the McCrickards were emerging from a shiny new Buick.

No ordinary mill hill couple, these McCrickards. That was clear from that first glimpse. If they were going to be our neighbors, where was the furniture? As far as I know, a real, honest-go-goodness moving van had never found its way to our neighborhood until the McCrickards arrived. Every move of which I had been aware had been made in an open, high side truck borrowed, in most cases, from T.E. Jones and Son Furniture.

Weather conditions were usually of no concern because most moves were for short distances – a matter of only a few streets or an occasional relocation across town to another mill village and another mill house. Short hauls. Quick trips back and forth until everything had been carried away to another house.

My own parents had made such a move in 1941, relocating just two houses away on Third Street, to one of the newer mill houses built in clusters of twos and fours at the ends of Second, Third and Fourth Streets. The Boggs family, the previous tenants, had made a major move to a new home on another mill hill more than 13 miles away in Greenville. So far away, my mother warned me, that I might never see Gary, their son my age, again. So far away, indeed, that I saw Gary only once in all the years after we had moved to the four-room house at the end of the street where he and his family had lived.

But the McCrickards' move would be a new experience for those of us who watched the goings on. And, indeed, most of us watched. Their belongings arrived in a big closed van and were unloaded by people apparently hired for just such chores.

The McCrickards also stood out because of what they had not brought to the house next door. They were apparently childless in a neighborhood where they would be surrounded by children. And childless families on the mill hill were unusual.

The author, left, and childhood friend Gary Boggs.

We had, from time to time, watched other childless couples move in. But invariably they were newlyweds and didn't remain childless for long. But the McCrickards did not seem to be newlyweds. Pretty and petite with coal-dark eyes, she already had turned prematurely gray. And he was a big man with big hands, with salt-and-pepper hair, a big smile and a deep bass voice that was remarkable in its gentle nature.

"What's your name?" she had asked after I had wandered from our house and stood in the shade of the oak tree that was so big it sheltered both our house and their new home.

"Wilton," I answered.

"Do you have a last name?"

"Browning."

"Well, Mr. Browning," she said with a smile. "Is your mother home?"

"Yes ma'am."

"Mother! Company!" I called out as the two of us, me and our new neighbor, stepped to the front porch and I reached for the screened door.

"My name is Cora Lee McCrickard and we're moving in next door and I just wanted to come say hello," she said.

That was different, too.

New neighbors normally didn't speak to the old-timers for a day or two. It was kind of a ritualistic checking out period for both the neighborhood and the newly arrived. Check out the kids, check to see whether the man of the house seems friendly or grumpy, check to see if they arrived with animals or not, check to see what kind of car and how old if they had a car at all.

Besides, the migration to the mill hills of the South had long ago been dominated by farmhands leaving the red clay fields in search of a more stable livelihood. And they brought with them a quietness, an aloofness that still was not uncommon on the mill hills of the 1940s and '50s. They were people with strong work ethic and with the understanding of an unspoken code that tolerated personal intrusions not at all.

That Buick, shiny and new, was the first hint that these McCrickards were going to be different. There were people on the mill hill who sometimes bought new cars, Chevys, Fords, an occasional Plymouth. Never Buicks. Too pretentious. Mr. Beacham, the mill super who lived in the big house on Fifth Street, drove a big Buick. So we certainly did not.

Indeed, for the first 12 years of my life, there was no car in our family. Not until my father bought a 1940 Plymouth sedan when it was almost 10 years old. That Plymouth was parked in our driveway the day the McCrickards arrived and emerged from their new Buick not 10 feet away.

And now, she had walked right into our house and introduced herself. That was very different.

It also was the start of a long friendship.

It was, as well, the start of the grandest era of iron-wheeled wagon building our mill hill ever knew. We became kind of the Detroit of the iron-wheeled wagon industry. And the McCrickards were an important part of that special time.

My first suspicion about the McCrickards had been accurate. These people had not spent much time laboring over looms and warps and frames, or in blowing off in the spinning room. Hadn't much lint been combed from their hair.

These weren't lintheads, these two. And for some of our neighbors, that meant they were outsiders who could not be redeemed by merely living next door.

In the world of big business, a world remote to most of us in those days, the owners of Easley Mill had contracted with the Whiting Textile Machine Co. to install a new generation of equipment and Mac had arrived as the mechanical engineer who would oversee the major renovation on behalf of the Whiting company. The job, done one careful segment at a time, would take months in a process that would limit the impact on cotton cloth production. And for all those months, the McCrickards would be our neighbors.

And for months, he would be overseeing an operation of tearing out-dated machinery from the four-story mill out beyond the ends of Third and Fourth Streets. And thus, creating a glut of iron wheels, the now obsolete cogs that drove the belts and pulleys that drove the textile machinery.

Iron-wheeled wagons were not an uncommon sight on the mill hill before the McCrickards arrived, but these would be their grandest days.

And those would be long, difficult months for third shift workers, those nocturnal souls who kept the mill humming from 11:00 at night until 7:00 in the morning and who were climbing into bed about the time the rest of us were arising, including those of us who cherished our moments of recklessly dashing down roughly paved streets in our own homemade iron-wheeled wagons.

None of us in those days had ever heard the roar of a small jet engine, but in retrospect that's what the noise was like. Those were the days when older kids used clothes pins to clip cardboard flaps to bicycle fender braces so that the spokes of the wheel spinning past the cardboard made a sound like that of an engine. But iron-wheeled wagons had a sound all their own.

Until the McCrickards arrived, the biggest problem in the construction of the wagons was the availability of wheels, the discarded 10-, 12- and 14-inch cogs that drove the machinery in the mills. Then suddenly, with the installation of the new equipment, wheels became plentiful, and sleepy third shift workers would have their daytime slumber disturbed for months.

One thing we learned in the construction of iron-wheeled wagons was patience. Steel rods, also discarded from textile machinery, served as the axles and were attached to two-by-four boards. But the ends of the steel rods had to be flattened to keep the wheels in place on the wagon, and that required long hours of pounding away at the end of the cold steel until we had left dime-shaped pit marks in the cement curbing along our streets. Those pitted curbs are still there, the only reminders of those marvelous wagons.

So plentiful were wheels while the McCrickards were our next door neighbors that had Neal and Ballard Tinsley been inclined, they could have become the Henry Fords of the iron-wheel set.

Tinsley wagons were the Cadillacs of the fleet. Most of the others were guided by straps attached to the front axle. But most of the Tinsley wagons had real honest-to-goodness steering wheels that worked. Broomsticks became the steering columns, and the manner in which leather straps were wrapped around the broomsticks made the wagon turn right and left and that wrapping of the strands of leather was a talent neither I nor most of my contemporaries ever mastered. Though we tried.

Neal and Ballard had an advantage a lot of us did not have. Their father, a man with dark eyes who seemed never to smile, and who seemed to have little patience for neighborhood children, was a second shift worker who also was an accomplished carpenter. And his talents were turned to wagon construction from time to time so that the Tinsley models were the class of the neighborhood.

It was an advantage that also showed up each spring when we launched by the dozens our home-made kites from the hillside in the pasture beside our house. Most of us also constructed our own kites of newspapers, homemade Ballard's self-rising flour paste and dry, brittle, light-weight reeds. But the Tinsleys' homemade kites always were better balanced, more perfect in design. They rose into the air easier and flew higher – so high they became tiny dots in the sky.

None of us, as far as I know, fully appreciated how special were those days, those final days of iron-wheeled wagons.

Mac McCrickard finished his work and the big moving van came once again to the house next door and the childless couple who had indirectly brought so much joy to a neighborhood full of children moved on to another town, another mill house, another job.

For another summer, those marvelous home-made wagons thundered down the hill on Third Street once again. And then they gradually disap-peared as their owners grew into other stages, as bicycles and, later, automobiles replaced those rumbling contraptions in our youthful affections.

Joe Young and I were on the cutting edge of those important life-style changes, the shift from iron-wheeled wagons to bicycles that came so gradually that none of us was aware of it, nor understood the social importance of the change.

Maybe the super, who lived in the big house on Fifth Street, drove the only Buick in our neighbor-hood, except for that marvelous car the McCrick-ards owned and kept polished. But no one owned bicycles as grand as the ones Joe and I cherished.

Joe, as I recall, got it all started the day he bought a pair of handlebar grips with foxtails attached. I countered that by putting double mirrors on my bicycle, which an elderly neighbor insisted upon calling a "wheel."

I went to red, white and blue plastic streamers attached to the handlebars of my bike and both Joe and I added mud flaps. His flaps had silver stars, mine reflectors.

But I wound up with the show bike that for a time was the envy of the neighborhood. Saving my earnings from my *Greenville News* paper route, I bought the top-of-the-line J.C. Higgins bicycle from Sears. It was a bicycle that had twin headlights, two rear-view mirrors, matching mud flaps with reflectors, chrome fenders, a luggage rack, a horn and it had double spring suspension at the front fork that helped cushion the ride.

It was a grand bicycle. But not very functional except for riding downhill and along level stretches of street. In most cases, it was so heavy it had to be pushed up hills.

But it was worth that inconvenience to own the grandest bicycle on the mill hill.

Not even the Tinsleys could come up with so grand a machine as that J.C. Higgins.

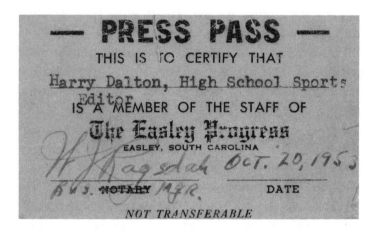

Photo courtesy of Ralph Hendrix

Harry Dalton's press pass showed he worked for The Easley Progess in 1953. At left, Harry Dalton, in center of front row, was team manager for the 1955 Easley High football team.

Ink in the Blood

In early May 1955, Harry Dalton signed my last high school annual and I signed his.

"Your pal, Scoop," he wrote there above his senior picture.

I was the only one who called Harry that. Harry, my best friend, lived in a mill house at the top of a steep hill on Eighth Street not far from the community baseball park where we both hoped to someday become stars. Harry was the sports editor of *The Green Wave*, the school newspaper at Easley High.

Harry knew I meant it as a compliment because the two of us were regular readers of Scoop Latimer, the sports editor of the *Greenville News*.

Both Harry and I worked with Scoop, though Scoop never knew. Harry kept the scorebook for most of the Easley High School basketball, baseball and football games and called the results in to the *News* promptly after each contest, though, as far as I know, he never talked directly to Latimer.

Still, there was a kinship there. There were days when Harry's two paragraphs on an Easley football game appeared on the same page as one of Scoop's columns, and that was good enough for us.

For my part, I spent seven years delivering the *News* to 105 mill hill customers. So, I took it as something of a sacred trust to see that Scoop – and the rest of the morning paper, for that matter – reached the readers on my route on time.

And for the moment, that too was good enough for us.

Mine was a job that gave me a special advantage over Harry, though. For most of those seven years, a truck arrived long before first light at the corner of Fifth Street and Fifth Avenue, across the street from the administrative office at the mill, and several bundles of newspapers were dropped off in the light of a street lamp, my 105 papers among them.

In the darkness of the early morning hour, in the light of the street lamp, I began a personal tradition that would last a lifetime – I sought out the sports page. Scoop had hooked me into that habit and for as long as I delivered the *Greenville News*, I read Scoop Latimer's column before I tossed the first paper onto a porch along my route.

Scoop knew on a first name basis a long list of sports figures who were legends in our young minds. He frequently wrote of telephone conversations with Jack Dempsey and Ty Cobb and Shoeless Joe Jackson and a dozen other names that were magic in those days.

Though I am certain Latimer did not know him

as a friend, for two days in the early 1950s, Scoop even wrote back-to-back columns on General George Custer. In remarkable prose, Scoop told us what a wonderful prize fighter Custer could have been.

Harry and I marveled over those two columns for days. It was that sort of thing that made Scoop so special. It never occurred to us that perhaps news was slow, and Scoop needed a couple of columns and along came this idea to do something on General George Armstrong Custer.

Harry didn't live long enough to learn of the legend behind the Custer columns, a secret I would discover a decade later when I returned home from the Air Force to go to work in the newsroom at the *Greenville News* at a desk beside long-time religion writer Gil Rowland.

"Scoop's office was right there," Gil told me one day in 1960 when I had asked about the late sports editor. Without bothering to look up from his work, Rowland had pointed over his shoulder to a cubicle then occupied by managing editor Carl Weimer.

"Read everything Scoop wrote, I reckon, for seven or eight years, until I joined the Air Force and left home," I said, making easy conversation with the friendly veteran newspaperman, who seemed in no mood to prolong this particular conversation. "But the columns that stick in my mind the most – and I don't know why except that they were so different from most things he wrote – were two he did on General Custer."

Suddenly interested, Rowland laughed loudly, one of those one-syllable bursts.

"Hah!"

"Funny how that happened," Rowland said, ignoring the work in front of him that moments earlier had seemed so riveting. "I was sitting right here, right where I am now, at this very desk. And I heard Scoop's phone ring. I didn't pay much attention to what he was saying. But he put the receiver down on his desk and started looking through the books in his office.

"He did that for a long time and he started getting frustrated and he turned and looked over this short partition here," said Rowland, turning in his swivel chair and putting his hand atop the five-foot tall partition. "And Scoop said, 'Hey, Gil. Ever hear of a fighter named Custer?'"

"Custer. Custer," Gil had repeated, searching his memory. "Sure haven't, Scoop. Only Custer I ever heard of got killed by the Indians at Little Big Horn."

"What was his name?" Latimer asked.

"George Armstrong Custer, I believe," Rowland said, telling the story with enthusiasm now, as though Scoop were there once again, just a few feet away. "He was a General. Fought in the Civil War on the Union side. Had long golden hair, they say. Got ambushed at Little Big Horn, and the Indians killed Custer and all his men."

"You still there?" Latimer had asked the voice on the other end of the phone line.

"The fighter you're calling about wouldn't be General George Armstrong Custer, would it?"

There was silence while Latimer listened to the voice on the other end of the line.

"Sorry it took so long. I thought you were calling about some prize fighter. Didn't think about General Custer when you called. General Custer got killed at Little Big Horn, you know. Everybody knows that."

Rowland had smiled at the memory. "Scoop was so embarrassed he spent the rest of the day doing research on Custer and wound up writing those two wonderful columns about what a great prize fighter the guy could have been.

"That was Scoop. Best ever, I reckon."

I reckoned so, too. And so did Harry.

But Harry was the "Scoop" I knew best, and we both tried to polish our budding journalism talents on the staff of the school newspaper, with Harry handling the sports coverage, while I did features and planned the pages.

But our journalism teacher, Miss Martha Davis, kept us reined in. None of that fancy writing at which Scoop was so skilled. Inverted pyramids, please, and just the four "Ws" and a "Why" and "How" tossed in occasionally for good measure.

And so Harry would write in restricted, right-to-the-point fashion:

The Easley High School Green Wave (Who) scored five touchdowns (How) in the second half Friday night

(When) on Brice Field (Where) and
went on to defeat Walhalla (What)
60-0.

Still, Harry seemed to do even that with a style, a flair all his own.

Harry and I shared a love for sports, but since Miss Davis had assigned me to write news stories and features, I felt an obligation, as I sat there beneath that street lamp each morning, to quickly scan the news pages as well. Occasionally, that was a mistake, for I discovered on those non-sports pages from time to time that there were things in this world more sensational, more frightening, than sports.

Like the morning in the foggy, eerie pre-dawn light that my eyes stopped on the story at the bottom of the front page that said the dismembered body of a man, believed to have been from Easley, had been discovered on a small sandbar island in the Pacolet River.

I read all the gruesome details and then began to wonder, since the corpse apparently was from Easley, if indeed he may not have been one of my subscribers.

For three days, while police authorities tried to identify the corpse before determining that he had lived at Glenwood Mill and not in my neighborhood and along my newspaper route, I worried about that. For a time, the 4:30 a.m. darkness in which I almost always began my daily rounds seemed darker still and more fearful. The shadows seemed to move, and when the porch swing at A.C. Walker's house suddenly stirred in the morning breeze and made a soft squeaking sound, I ran most of a block before regaining my nerve.

None of that would have been as frightening had it happened later in my long career as the carrier along the "front side" at Easley Mill. Because for the last several years in which I earned my spending money as the man who got Scoop's columns to 105 waiting customers, I had a welcome companion. The Coxes' collie puppy, Rex, had grown to adulthood. And at 4 every morning, as though he could tell time, Rex met me at my door and accompanied me around my paper route.

My mother always said she could keep up with my morning progress by sound – the barking of the dogs along my route, greetings that Rex mostly ignored.

He was a wonderful companion, and when strange dogs appeared from the dark shadows, stirred from their sleep by my passing, Rex always walked between me and the other dogs, never growling without cause, never threatening, but always there.

Rex wasn't a fighter by nature, but one of our tranquil strolls through the morning was shattered the day he was attacked by a neighboring dog in a fight so vicious that the owner of the attacking dog was awakened. Angered by Rex' success against his two younger dogs, he followed the same trail of barking dogs in which my mother took comfort. He pumped a series of .22 bullets into my friend who escaped badly wounded. I searched for my canine friend through the morning without success and for five days made my deliveries alone and lonesome. Almost a week later, Rex dragged himself home. Five bullets were taken from his body and he struggled for life as the Cox family carefully nursed him back from near death.

And there was an emptiness inside as I delivered 104 copies of the *Greenville News* and worried about whether my friend would make it through this crisis. I had protested the vicious attack the only way I knew, by refusing to continue the *News* subscription to the customer who had tried to kill my special friend.

That reaction not taken lightly by my former customer who again and again asked me to continue his paper and who finally phoned in his complaint to Mr. Stephenson, my route supervisor.

"He says you refuse to deliver his paper," Mr. Stephenson said that day after school when he arrived at my house. "Said he had always paid his bill on time and can't understand why you won't deliver the paper to his house."

"He understands," I told my boss, then explained how important Rex had become in my life, about the bond we had formed and that Rex had only joined the dog fight when he feared I was being threatened.

"If it's all right with you," I said when I had finished explaining to Mr. Stephenson, "I'd just as soon never deliver a paper to that man again."

"And I hope you never will," my boss said, then drove away.

And I never did. Though when the man who shot Rex was drafted for the Korean War, he came to my house to tell me he was sorry he had retaliated against the dog.

But the disenfranchised customer had spoken the truth when he had told my boss that he had always promptly paid his bill. Mill hill folks always paid their bills. Thirty-five cents a week, every week, and every Friday afternoon I made the rounds on my route collecting the weekly fee from first-shift workers, and on Saturday mornings and early afternoon collecting from second- and third-shift hands.

And every Friday, when I knocked on Mr. Walker's door on Fourth Street, the tall, friendly, mustachioed man always opened the door and said, "I'll bet you're here to clack."

Months earlier, he had insisted that I never clearly said that "I'd like to collect," but that it came out, "I'd like to clack." And for a long time he had said, "Well, Wilton, go ahead and clack."

"I'll bet you're here to clack," he said again and again, always paying, always with the exact change.

One-hundred-four customers, 102 doors to knock on every week. One customer left the 35 cents under a doormat every Saturday morning, never missing a Saturday, and one other paid once a month.

It's the sort of thing one learned delivering papers on the mill hill. Folks honored their financial obligations, 35 cents at a time.

Which seemed to me to be a reasonable sum for the privilege of reading Scoop Latimer every day.

Photo courtesy of the Dalton Family

Harry Dalton, center, in 1954, with brother Dennis, right, and friend "Pee Wee" Waldrop.

Harry

Had they chosen to bury Harry over there atop the next hill, the one nearer the highway, there beneath the old water oak, instead of here in the family plot near the back of the cemetery, it would have pleased Harry.

Why, from over there, from beneath the old water oak, one almost could see Underwood Field, the old mill village ballpark. What's left of it. Harry would have liked that.

Harry Dalton. My best friend in those years of growing and dreaming. Kindred souls, we were. Sons of the mill hill, both of us. A year's difference in our ages. Harry's parents had been forced to postpone his enrollment in school only weeks before he was scheduled to begin the first grade at West End Elementary. Thus, in a sense, Harry, a year older, had waited for me and we had been classmates since the day we took our seats side-by-side at too-large desks in Miss Carolyn Smith's first grade classroom all those years ago. Both of us were in love with baseball and both destined to dream of becoming sports writers, just like Scoop

Latimer and Anthon Foy and Red Canup and Jake Penland, writers who would become our heroes, our Keats, our Faulkners.

In both baseball and in those laborious early high school sports stories through which we struggled, Harry was more talented than I. I can tell you that without reservation, with the heart of an innocent, with modesty no consideration, certain that it is the truth.

But Harry died a long time ago.

I was there. Not in the moment of his dying, but shortly before death came, gently I am told. And I was there with Curtiss Atkins and Larry Bagwell and the rest, to accompany Harry as his fuzzy-cheeked pallbearers to that spot on the hillside now marked by a tiny slab of marble.

But Harry is not dead. Hasn't been in my memory for all these years. I still can feel his frail, bony right hand squeezing mine as he looked up through tired eyes from his hospital bed. And though the struggles with his failing heart had robbed him of his strength, he smiled.

"This is the summer we were going to the All-Star game. Remember?" he had said so softly that only I could have heard.

"Yeah, Harry. You'd better rest now."

He found strength to squeeze my hand harder.

"It's going to be in Washington, where the Senators play. I wrote away for our tickets, you know. But getting them's a long shot. Still, we could have gone, couldn't we? Wouldn't it have been something, seeing Pee Wee and Musial and all the rest?"

"Yeah. That've been something," I said, sharing his dream, worrying about my best friend.

"Still want to be a writer? A sports writer?"

"I don't know, Harry. I guess."

"You will. I know you will." He swallowed hard, his drawn, ancient-looking teenage face momentarily masked in pain. Then, the smile came back, a flicker at a time, and he still held my hand.

"Promise me something."

"Sure, Harry. Anything."

"Promise me you'll be a sports writer. And some day when you go to cover the all-star game, and you walk into that dressing room to talk to Pee Wee and Stan and the others, and when you go to the press box and open your scorebook, remember me. Remember that we were going to be there together."

Harry looked into my eyes. I turned away, as I lost the fight to control my emotions.

"You and me, Wilt," he said, the start of a laugh turning to a noisy, ragged cough instead. "The two best sports writers who ever lived."

"You and me, Harry."

The burning in my eyes, the hurting in my chest was still oppressive, and still I looked away.

"Hey," he said, pulling at my hand. "You gotta promise."

"I promise."

Now, it would be poetic to tell you, children,

that I became a sports writer to keep that promise to my dying friend. Poetic, but an exaggeration.

But, I did make it as a sports writer to the All-Star game. I did walk among the stars in the National League dressing room, though by then Musial and Reese and the others had aged into retirement. I did take my assigned seat in the press box, and I did open my scorebook to dutifully enter there the hits, runs and errors.

And I did think of Harry, and I wished he could have been there with me. Maybe even instead of me.

But, I've always thought of Harry.

Harry, you must understand, taught us about death at a time in our lives when death seemed such a remote possibility, at a time when we were going to live forever, when youth was eternal, just one doubleheader after another, endless.

So unfair that Harry would be the teacher of that bitter lesson.

Look, Harry could play baseball, though he was a senior in high school before he pushed the team's scorebook into my hands with instructions to call the *Greenville News* and the *Anderson Independent* when the game had ended. He walked away to the gym and appeared a short time later, looking grand indeed in his white flannel baseball uniform with "Green Wave" across the chest and with his favorite number "11" on his back.

"Harry, the heart," I had said, worrying about my friend.

"What about the heart?" he asked, turning suddenly more hostile than I had ever known Harry to be.

"Don't play games, Harry. Not with me." I knew his mortal secret, and now he knew I knew. Harry's mother and mine worked together in the spinning room at the mill on the second shift. And only a few weeks into our senior year in high school, my mother had broken the news at breakfast one morning.

"Harry's mother says Harry's sick," she had said.

"I was with him yesterday," I had protested. "Same old Harry, seemed to me."

"Weak heart. They say he has to be very careful. And he isn't likely to live a long time. I just thought you ought to know."

And now, there he was, trotting to the hole at second base, fielding a grounder and with one wonderful, beautiful, perfect motion throwing to first just the way Rizzuto would have done it.

Except better, in my mind. "Take it easy, Harry," I wanted to cry out, but didn't.

"Harry, the heart," I would protest again.

"I know. But let's don't talk about that now. Let me have this season, just this one season and I'll be happy," he had said, now happier than I had ever seen him.

Harry had that one season. That one grand, glorious season. No one in our town ever played second base more grandly, more perfectly.

Nor enjoyed it more.

Nor paid more dearly for the privilege. It killed Harry.

We buried Harry there, in my opinion atop the wrong hill, on the very day they played the All-Star game in Washington, the day Harry and I were supposed to be there.

No Place for Strangers

As I look back now, I realize that there were a lot of unwritten codes involved with living on the mill hills of the South, and the neighborhood of my youth was no exception.

As I had learned from my paper route, lintheads, even the ones who never showed up in Sunday School, paid their bills. Honest people. People who honored their commitments. People who kept their word. The kind of people who ordered groceries by phone, charged it and always paid when payday rolled around. People who trusted their neighbors so much they never locked their doors, nor ever needed to. People for whom a handshake really was as binding as a signed contract. And almost to a person, they kept the loosely translated Christian version of the Sabbath. Sundays on a mill hill were peaceful times. No one cut grass or worked the Victory Gardens, many of which continued to be planted spring after spring though the war had ended a long time ago. And the play of children was more subdued, their noisy enthusiasms muted in the honoring of the weekly holy day.

But there was another code none of us talked much about and it had to do with whatever scoundrels were among us. Though children were brought inside when mad dogs and drunks were about, mill hill drunks always kept their distance from families such as ours and most others on the mill hill, never intruding, though we came to understand that there were some mean drunks among us who occasionally visited their violence upon wives and other members of their families.

It was a side of mill hill life of which not many of us who grew up there in the 1940s and '50s were aware, though from time to time we would see that ragged group of men with strangely bulging pockets walk past our house, take a path through the pasture that adjoined our yard and disappear into the distant woods from which they would reappear in the shank of the evening in drunken conditions, their pockets no longer bulging.

"Rough? Certainly it was a rough place, the mill hill," Juber Hairston said long after he had gotten religion and had personally given up the rough life, and years after he had retired from Easley Mill.

"You remember where you used to get your haircut?" he asked.

Upstairs, over the hardware store on Main Street, in L.A. Gilstrap's barber shop, I answered. Spent many a Saturday there, waiting my turn, sitting near the open second-story window watching long trains rumble past on the main Washington-to-Atlanta Southern Railway line that dissected our town, dreaming about distant destinations where grown men played baseball, finding dreamy magic in the very name of that daily passenger train, the Southern Crescent. I didn't bother to tell him that there were as well times that I got my hair cut for 25 cents by Squalie Merck on his back porch on Second Street.

"That's what I mean," Juber said. "You went to a fancy place in town to get your hair cut. Used to go to Poe Mill myself. And to get to the barber shop at Poe Mill, you had to walk through what we called the Ape Yard. Only two ways to get through the Ape Yard — run or fight.

"But there was no place tougher than Easley Mill in my time," Hairston said. In his young adulthood, Hairston was a regular patron at a beer joint in a dark building cut into the red earth of a hillside on Fifth Street not far from the administrative offices at the mill, but mercifully removed from the mill village itself. Unmercifully, not removed far enough, because generation after generation of school children had to daily walk past the building with the bad reputation on their way to and from West End Elementary.

"No place for strangers," Juber said of the old watering hole that no longer exists.

"Weren't supposed to sell liquor there, but they did. For 50 cents, they'd fill up a Coca-Cola bottle.

Just in case somebody came nosing around, it'd look like we were all sitting there drinking Coca-Colas. Gentlemen, enjoying dopes, you know.

"But one night, a stranger walked in."

He almost didn't walk out.

In what must have been something like a barroom scene from an old Western movie, the place grew silent when the stranger came through the door. No one spoke. Every patron turned to look.

The stranger walked in from the daylight and moved across the room to the old service counter that served as a bar. "Any way a man can get a drink of liquor here?" the stranger asked, breaking the silence.

"No sir, not here," the owner answered.

"I was told I could find something here," the stranger pressed.

"Somebody told you wrong. You can find a beer here, but that's all."

"Got a taste for whiskey myself," the stranger said.

The owner looked about the dimly lighted room. A big man in the corner nodded. One nod of the head that the stranger had not seen, a signal meant only for the owner and those gathered at the neighborhood watering hole. Without further discussion, the operator of the place produced an empty Coca-Cola bottle from beneath the counter and, in clear view of all the regular customers, filled it with liquor nearly the color of the soft drink for which the bottle had been intended.

"That'll be four bits," the unsmiling operator said, as he pushed the newly filled soft drink bottle across the counter to the stranger.

The stranger slapped a shiny 50-cent piece down noisily, wiped the top of the bottle with the palm of his hand and brought the container to his mouth.

Before he could take the first swallow, he felt the sharp, cold steel of a knife pressed against the side of his neck and felt the presence of a big man at his back.

A handful of regular customers moved close and the big man with the big knife spoke softly but firmly.

"Drink every drop of it, stranger," he said. "Or die."

Nothing moved except the suddenly frightened eyes of the stranger who looked left and then right into one unsmiling face and then another. He took the reasonable option, brought the Coca-Cola bottle once again to his mouth and drank down the contents.

"That's good," the big man with the big knife said approvingly. "Now who the hell are you?"

"Too bad they had to do that to that guy," Juber said. "He was just a stranger in town looking for some liquor. Didn't mean no harm to anybody. But no way we could take a chance. No way of knowing when an undercover agent was going to show up."

The operators of the mill must have known

that it was reasonable to expect that among the several hundred people employed on the three shifts there would be those, exceptions though they may be, who would frequent such places, or who would occasionally wander into the woods near Oates Cemetery for a purpose no more noble than the consumption of beer and whiskey. For the most part, though, drinking never became much of a community problem because of a rule that was brilliant in its simplicity:

"You get drunk and cause a fuss on Saturday night," Juber said, "and Monday'd be moving day."

There was no appeal, no trial by jury. No presumption of innocence. Nothing but a summons to the super's office on Monday morning to answer for the binge of Saturday night. Final. Effective. Perhaps because that threat lingered there at the bottom of every can of beer and the bottom of every "dope" bottle filled with whiskey, only once did I personally encounter a drunken neighbor. It happened just before sunup one Sunday morning when I made the turn onto Third Street on my regular rounds of delivering the *Greenville News.*

In the half-light of the early hour, I could make out in the distance the familiar figure of Mr. Hopkins, a neighbor, who was strolling along the street in uncertain steps.

"Hey, boy!" he called out when he came close.

"Good morning, Mr. Hopkins," I answered.

"You know me?" He seemed confused.

"Certainly I know you, Mr. Hopkins."

"Do I know you?" he asked, his speech slurred.

"Yessir, I think so."

"Well, if you know me and I know you," he began in the strange logic of the drunk, "would you tell me something else?"

"Sure."

"Where do I live?"

"Right there," I answered, pointing to the four-room house exactly like my own home, the house not 100 feet from where we stood on the pleasant early morning.

He began to weep. "I'm so happy," he said through his tears. "I thought I was lost."

"Oh, no sir," I tried to console him. "Can I help you get home?"

"Certainly not," he said somewhat indignantly, suddenly no longer weeping. "I know where I am, thank you very much." And he was gone, climbing as gracefully as he could under the conditions the long flight of steps leading to the front porch of the house in which he lived with a daughter and grandson and a dog that walked on only his two front legs, a strange improvisation the animal gallantly developed after being run over by an automobile and left partially paralyzed.

There also were among our neighbors those who, it was said, had once been inclined to drink but who had gotten religion or gotten frightened, or both, and had given up strong spirits. Still they carried the marks of a wayward life, a scar here, a broken marriage there, though divorce was rare in our community where God and the mill super were feared above all else.

And most of the drinking was the socially accepted kind, soft drinks purchased for a nickle apiece off the dope wagon that made its way regularly through the mill. Or a dope bought at the mill canteen, which was a sandwich and hot dog stand known as the junk, or from the dope box at McCoy's Grocery on Fifth Street.

On the mill hill, it was a blessed age of innocence, even for a lot of adults who attached no social significance to our word for soft drinks – dopes – though there were those who would later tie the colloquialism to the "Coca" in Coca-Cola, a suggestion that when the soft drink first hit the market perhaps the secret ingredient that made the famous product such an instant hit was just a hint of cocaine.

And so it was that the regulars at the neighborhood drink house poured their liquor into dope bottles, just in case some stranger happened by. Just gentlemen having a dope or two, these scoundrels among us, the men not long on friendly conversation, men more inclined to fight first, or slash the throat of a stranger and ask questions later.

Indeed, from time to time, we would hear tales of disagreements that had simmered into open brawls among adults, but in most cases, most of the violence, primarily childhood fights, was left to the pre-teens growing up on the mill hill.

None of us was excused.

Rodney Brown became my own personal tormentor in those early years at West End Elementary School, where teachers sought to broaden the horizons of those of us growing up on the mill hill, on which most people had never traveled beyond the state line.

But Rodney was more interested in sharpening his pugilistic skills at my expense than in studying world history. A few months younger but more stoutly built than I, Rodney took delight in ambushing me daily on my long walks home in the afternoons.

And for a lot of days, I arrived home battered and bruised to receive fresh encouragement from my father, a peaceful man who seemed to have no fear and who apparently expected me to have none.

But he must have known there was fear within my heart and for days I tried without success to alter my route home in efforts to elude Rodney Brown. Rodney seemed to know instinctively if I walked home along the railroad tracks that ran from back of West End Elementary to Easley Mill as a spur of that wonderful Southern Railway line that ran through town. Or, if I took the long way home along First Street, Rodney always was there.

My torment ended abruptly on a day on which I resolved to fight back and, indeed, on a day on which I steeled my nerves and purposely took the most direct route home, one that took me across the corner of the Browns' yard and along the side of their house.

As I suspected, Rodney was waiting for me there, just out of sight, and when he leaped from his hiding place and into my path, I stood my ground. He swung, as he always did, and missed, as he almost never did, as I ducked away. Wildly, blindly I returned the aggression and with one swing knocked free Rodney's two large upper front teeth. Bloodied, he ran crying into his house.

I continued my walk home suddenly conscious of a most wonderfully sweet contentment, feeling that I had learned something about bravery.

"Did you have a good day?" my father asked when I arrived home.

"Sure did."

Before the sun had gone down on that perfect day, Rodney's father had come knocking at our front door to inform my dad that he was raising a bully, that my family would be expected to pay for any dental work Rodney's condition required.

They argued about that, and once again my father seemed to be perfectly in control of the situation, politely concerned about Rodney's problem but firmly standing his ground and disavowing any liability. At one point, my father even had secretly winked at me when the exchange had become more pointed.

Rodney's father finally left, but not before salvaging whatever consolation he could.

"You'd better tell your boy to stay out of our yard and to leave Rodney alone," he said, his face seemingly more red with anger than it had been.

"Well, a dad'll do what a dad has to do, won't he?" my father had responded. "I'll have a talk with my boy right away. Now, Wilton, you will stay out of Mr. Brown's yard, won't you? And I expect you to quit beating Rodney up the way you have."

There was a wonderfully proud smile on my father's face as he said it. We both knew that this was a scolding without heart, meant more for the ears of the angry Mr. Brown than for my father's son.

"I won't go into their yard," I promised, "and I promise to leave Rodney alone from now on."

And I did. And Rodney never again waited in ambush for me.

Still, it was an incident that remained in my memory, a reminder, like the drunks and the strangers among us, that there were hard lessons to be learned in growing up on the mill hill.

But some lessons were more difficult than others. It was on the mill hill that even the youngest among us learned how fragile life can be.

If the mill hill was, in the late '40s and through the '50s, the wonderful place of growing up that I knew it to be, it was at the same time a place of difficult existence for animals. Part of that grew out of an unreasonable fear of the unknown.

There were, of course, no leash laws or inoculation rules for pets who shared our homes and with

Family pictures. Upper right, the author with his first car, around 1942. Upper left, the author plays marbles, around 1941. At left, sister Doris Ann Browning, in the late '40s. Below, Marlene Browning, in the late '40s.

the heat of late summer would come the annual fear of dogs gone mad. Some years were more frightful than others, and once word had spread that mad dogs were about, there developed groups of armed vigilantes who roamed the streets looking for monsters most of us saw only in our imaginations – once loving, friendly pets grotesquely changed by an illness, snarling, red-eyed, foaming at the mouth. Death on four legs. The armed men roamed about, slaughtering dogs that were running free, killing them by the dozens, most without cause, most free of rabies.

Those were dreadful days to be a boy in love with a friendly dog.

Even in months when mad dogs were not said to be roaming our neighborhood, dogs were occasionally selectively destroyed, a bitterness that more than once touched our family.

Before I had ever owned one, I fell in love with collie dogs in the pages of my second grade reader where there was the story of Carlo, the Collie. And in an early winter when Santa was still an important part of my own imagination, I asked for a collie for Christmas. I would name it Carlo.

Long before sunrise that Christmas morning, the yelping of a puppy awakened me and the joy we both shared at first meeting still lives in my memory, the softness of the puppy's fuzzy coat, puppy feet so large for such a small creature he seemed to trip over them, the white tip at the end of his tail making rapid arcs as he wagged out his friendship, a small white blaze on his nose that made him even more special, even the freshness of Carlo's breath as he snuggled close to me.

Carlo and I grew together, loving each other, spending long days running side-by-side across the field that was the pasture beside our house. Perfect friends.

What I did not fully appreciate was that Carlo was rare on the mill hill. He was a collie through and through, with the coloring of Lassie and the big, bushy white collar so typical of his breed. The long, noble nose. Ears that stood erect except when I patted his head. A collie more beautiful than Lassie. All the other dogs in our neighborhood were mongrels, lovable, wonderful mixtures of terrier and beagle and hound and such. But mongrels nonetheless.

Made no difference to me, nor to Carlo as far as I could tell. His own best buddy was part blue-tick hound, part something else that suffered occasionally from the mange, and the German Shepherd that belonged to Alvoid Galloway next door.

Though I was too young to understand it at the time, Alvoid's dog became the target of a hired killer. Because the shepherd had fought with a neighbor's dog, a feeble-minded teenager was paid a few dollars to toss poisoned meat into the Galloway's yard. But most of it landed on our side of the fence. Alvoid's shepherd survived. Carlo did not.

He lay dead when I came to call him to play the

next morning, his legs stiff, his eyes fixed in a morbid stare. The veterinarian said the dog that loved me so much had eaten food laced with strychnine. For a long time, growing up on the mill hill seemed no more a paradise.

Some of us learned about death in other ways, as well. Among the first aspects of mill hill life, as I knew it, to come to an end was the autumn ritual of hog killing.

Hogs belonging to families on our side of the mill hill were raised in wooden pens made of rough saw mill slabs and placed in the shade of big oak trees in a grove between the end of Second Street and Pendleton Street.

Hogs weren't easy to love, not like Penny, our cow, who grazed in the pasture beside our house and came occasionally to push her head between the top two strands of barbed wire so that we could more easily rub her nose, feeling the softness of the fur between her big brown eyes.

Penny supplied a lot of our dairy needs, until a particularly abundant summer crop of bitterweed made her milk undrinkable and Penny was sold to some uncertain future.

But hogs weren't friendly like Penny had been. And their fur was wiry, their moods grumpy, their appetites out of control so that when we poured the mixture of table leftovers and hog feed down the chute and into the trough, much of the daily serving wound up on the snout of the growing animal.

We gave our cow a name to match the color of her coat. We never named our pigs. Still, we were taught to treat them with respect, to see to their daily needs of food and water.

My father was a non-violent man and perhaps that is one of the reasons we never raised more than two or three hogs, as I can recall, in all the years we lived at Easley Mill a short walk from the grove where tin-roofed slab sheds stood scattered about in the shade.

Indeed, by the time my generation came along, hog-raising was already a dying activity on the mill hill, so that I witnessed the ritual only one time.

These days, I presume, hogs are almost never raised singly, but on large corporate farms and shipped to packing houses for their slaughter. But late fall when the fresh meat would be naturally chilled by the weather was hog-killing time on the mill hill, a time when there was a predictable chill on the air and most of the leaves had fallen from the big oaks that had for a summer sheltered these animals that we owned.

The last such ritual in which my immediate family participated came on a cold day, a day on which there was little light conversation at the breakfast table, a Saturday on which my father would be home from the mill. A day, I realize now, that must have been a difficult one for him.

I had trailed behind him as we made our way to the pen in which our own pig had grown large and heavy and noisy. And there, my father had told me to remain some distance away and not to look at what was about to happen.

From beneath a distant oak, I watched my father and mother silently preparing for a ritual that must have taken place for hundreds of years. Two large black wash pots were filled with water and wood and coal was lighted beneath each so that smoke curled into the wintery air.

Finally, my father nodded and mother came to stand with me, hugging me to her, suggesting that I turn away. But I watched as my father raised his .22 rifle to his shoulder and rested the barrel of the weapon on one of the rough slaps of the pen. A shot rang out, and the hog that I had helped feed for the last year crashed to the wooden floor on which he had spent his life, and was still.

My father removed the clip from his rifle. He seemed shaken, more somber than I had ever known him to be. And now he used a crowbar to remove the slabs that formed one of the four walls. Even the boards seemed to cry out in protest, the creaking of rusty nails being pried from stout timber seeming to scream.

Other adults whom I did not know arrived, and silently, quickly, everyone became engrossed in the business of harvesting the meat that would come to our table in the coming months as bacon and pork chops and roasts and cracklin' for our cornbread.

This was the gift of food for our table. And

perhaps in introducing their young son to this ancient ritual, there was an assumption that some day I too would bring food to my own table and to my own family in just such a manner.

My own father had had little enthusiasm for such time-honored ritual, and we never again raised pigs in the pen in the grove of big oaks. The three wooden slabs lay for years on the ground where they had fallen to by father's crowbar, and weeds grew where the pork had been rendered after the hog had been dipped in the big black wash pots filled with steaming water to remove the bristly hair.

"You know, I hear they have good meat down at Welborn's," my mother said softly to my father a few days later. And for all the years that came after that, we bought our pork, beef and poultry from the store in the forks of the road where Heyward Harris took the orders by phone, personally selected the cuts of meat for his customers and slipped the bill beneath a clip on his folding credit board.

When the early chill of winter came again, none of us felt sadness that an ancient ritual no longer was part of our lives.

Credit
Where Credit Is Due

A lot of folks discovered Welborn's about the time we did and though Claude Welborn had long ago sold the country grocery business to Marion Harris, folks still continued to call it Welborn's from force of habit.

Formally, once Claude Welborn retired to the big white house in Anderson County the store became Pickensville Grocery and Feed. But we weren't ones to stand on formality, and it still was Welborn's to us.

For as long as Claude Welborn had owned the store in the Pickensville community, it had been mostly a business catering to rural folks. Hundred-pound bags of cow and hog feed were stored in the basement along with endless cases of bath and hand soap and for years a black man named James and his wife worked there in the cool darkness and walked home in the long shadows of summer days to a shack they shared three miles away.

Welborn's began to prosper when the Harrises

took over – Marion, the owner, and Heyward, his brother who ran the place and who scribbled phoned-in grocery orders onto small pads so that there were times that only he could read what had been written there.

Yet he filled every order as if it were his own, selecting the most red, firm tomatoes, choosing cuts of beef for its quality and then sending the order on its way in store-owned delivery trucks. It was not a very adventuresome job, delivering groceries, but one that was coveted by the handful of employees, because it provided relief from the produce and meat departments and from bagging groceries on Friday afternoons and on Saturdays.

Heyward Harris was a man with a keen memory for matters of importance to his customers. "You've got to remember that the Browns want Chase & Sanborn coffee and not Maxwell House," he scolded one employee who had arrived at one of two check-out counters with the good-to-the-last-drop brand. "It's the Owenses who want you to bring them Maxwell House. Think you can remember that?"

Groceries were packed for travel with care, so that loaves of bread arrived uncrushed and vegetables unbruised. Some of them even were delivered for a time in a big black Cadillac, a vehicle borrowed from the used car lot next door after one of two open-bed trucks used for deliveries failed to negotiate a curve in Anderson County, left the road, crashed and scattered groceries across the rural landscape.

Many of the regular weekly orders were delivered while the customers were at work in the mill and their homes were unattended. Our directions were to call out as we arrived at the back door of a customer's home, which would always be unlocked. If nobody was home, it was the duty of the delivery person to make sure perishable items – such as milk, eggs and meats – were placed in the refrigerator.

Old-fashioned service. Dependable service.

Williams Grocery in the center of town also offered delivery service, but Welborn's offered the best meat at the best prices around and thus cornered the market on our side of town.

Heyward Harris made regular trips to Hugheys' wholesale meat locker on Greenville Highway to personally select huge sides of beef and cuts of pork that would find their way into the coolers at his store at Pickensville. And he presided over the carving of cuts that would become the best hamburger in town and over the selection of pork shoulders that would be ground and mixed with a savory selection of herbs and spices – Heyward's own secret recipe – that would become the most sought-after pork sausage in town.

For years, Ponders' Ice Cream Parlor on Main Street ordered its ground beef from Welborn's in 10-pound packages and with it created the best chili-and-onion hamburgers in the South. Welborn's closed its doors a year before Easley Mill shut down, and the Ponders long ago sold the ice

An evening in the ice cream parlor, 1957.

cream parlor to Joe Lesley, who renamed the place "Joe's" and has carried on the hamburger tradition to this day.

Indeed, the ice cream parlor, the gathering place for high school juniors and seniors for as long as there has been an Easley High School, is one of the last reminders of the way life used to be for mill hill folks. The only concession Lesley, and Ponders before him, has made to the modern world is linoleum floors where sweet-smelling sawdust floors once were.

For a lot of years, old sawdust was swept out of the ice cream parlor once a week, after the close on Saturday night, and fresh sawdust scattered in its place, a tradition that would have made finding the best hamburgers in the South an easy matter for strangers in town who needed only to follow the trail of dusty shavings along the Main Street sidewalks to the doors of what now is simply known as Joe's.

Old-timers still call it the ice cream parlor.

Williams Grocery, on the other hand, served Miss Mae Jones' hot dog stand on the other end of Main Street in a small establishment beside Luke's Taxi stand. There were wonderful aromas that came from that small eatery where on Saturday afternoon after the western movie and the *Black Widow* serial had been run at the Lyric Theater, a chili hot dog and Dr. Pepper costing a total of less than 25 cents topped off the day.

I am not certain which of the two grocery

competitors first introduced a delivery service, but it was a strategic marketplace move that would not have been possible until the mid- to late-1930s when the cotton mills joined most of the rest of the country on the silver standard.

There is the shell of an old store building still standing at the corner of Fifth Street and Seventh Avenue at Easley Mill that once was McCoy's Grocery, which also belatedly had delivery service. It had carried other names over its history, but Pat McCoy had been the last to operate a successful grocery business there. But McCoy's, a store restricted by its small size, would wind up yielding its share of the market – even on the mill hill – to Welborn's and Williams' just as those two establishments would, by the late 1950s, begin to fade against the pressure of Winn-Dixie and other chain supermarkets. Williams' would close its doors first when shopping centers sprang from the countryside where the new Highway 123 bypass now runs, thus diverting traffic from the center of town, and Welborn's would finally yield to the times in 1989, a year in which Heyward retired and Marion, who after the age of 40 took up tennis and became a nationally ranked player, died.

But McCoy's, standing now only as a shell, is the last vestige of the old company store operation that stood just off-center from the middle of the mill village. Gone now are virtually all traces of at least three other buildings that stood near the old store and once housed other company establishments, including a barber shop, feed store and clothing store, all of which accepted as payment script issued by the mill as salary.

The form of payment was as individual as the mill companies themselves. Easley Mill paid in paper script, Brandon and Woodside at Greenville in coupons and brass chits respectively. Cash through the early half of mill hill existence was rare, though there were those anxious to serve as currency exchangers. About 80 cents in cold cash would buy a dollar's worth of script.

When the mill began paying in cash, in small brown envelopes in the case of Easley Mill, a lot of things began to change in our neighborhood and those like them scattered across the South. For the first time, mill hands had an honest-to-goodness choice of where the necessities of life would be purchased, and Welborn's Grocery and Williams' Grocery were there with the delivery trucks to cash in and to bring, if only marginally, a life more full to the mill hill.

Cash, and the credit for which the reliable folks on the mill hill could qualify, also brought Sears-Roebuck and Co., and the mail order business to the mill hill in a big way. Cars still were the exception rather than the rule for most mill hill families through World War II, but Sears, like Williams and Welborn, was ready to bring the world to the villages through the dreamy pages of its mail order catalogs.

Slowly, those wonderful people with heads

made dusty each day with cotton dust and many with cheeks filled with tobacco or snuff were becoming factors in the marketplaces of big business without even knowing it. Life on the mill hill changed one modest dream at a time.

What did not change for a long time was the presence of spittoons along the hardwood floors at the mill and the "Do Not Spit on the Floor" signs. Still, expert tobacco chewers regularly oiled the gears that drove the machinery with well-placed tobacco juice. There was pride involved even in that.

Though we who would make up the first generation to escape the cotton mills of the South in large numbers were watching without understanding a series of irrevocable changes in a way of life, indeed much already had changed by the time we came along as the final set of children to understand the difference in toys, agates and steelies in the games of marbles we played beneath the big oak tree in our yard.

What we missed was substantial. Not only did we come along after the script years and company stores, we also arrived too late to hear Sousa played on the Fourth of July by people who worked in the spinning rooms, weave rooms and card rooms of the big cotton manufacturing plants.

Lost now from the family album back home on the mill hill is a fading picture of Irvin McNeely standing beside a small lad sitting on the right front fender of McNeely's A-Model Ford. McNeely was a friendly man who tantalized small children with tales of long trips through the countryside to "Big Greenville," which, most of us discovered later in life, really was not so big at all.

But McNeely also had been a trumpet player in the Glenwood Mill band and he still practiced regularly expecting, like Juber Hairston and Paul Rampey would anticipate the revival of baseball on the mill hill, a mustering of musicians once again. McNeely had been a part of that wonderful time in the teens and 20s when the mills outfitted their musicians with matching uniforms and constructed bandstands on lawns near the plant, structures long ago torn down and hauled away in pieces.

Now, with the mills closing one by one, even those days are lost to the memory to all but the very oldest. McNeely himself died a long time ago, his trumpet and his shiny A-Model lost to the ages as well.

No one calls in grocery orders to Welborn's anymore.

Growing up on mill hill. Top
left, the author, around 1942.
Top right, the author, around
1943. Bottom, the author and
sister Marlene, around 1942.

Warm Morning Winters

"Hey, mister. What ya doing?" I asked the man who was pouring a gray floury mixture into a shallow, square wooden tub, then adding sand and water and stirring the recipe together with a hoe with holes in it.

"Fixin' to mix some mortar," he said.

"Then what ya going to do?"

"Brick up your house."

"Mind if I watch?" I asked. Had the man and his mortar arrived a few years earlier, I might not have been so casual about this change in our lives. I had spent a lot of hours all alone pushing bricks through the dirt beneath our house pretending they were cars and that the imaginary town there in the dusty red clay could be any place I wanted it to be. It could be Brooklyn, where the Dodgers played, though I had no idea how Brooklyn really looked. Or Boston, where the Braves played. Over there, at the base of that little mound, could be Ebbets Field that, I thought, must look something like the ball park on the back side of the mill hill where the mill team played.

But I had changed. I was almost 10 years old now, and my leisure time needs had changed as well. I no longer needed to push imaginary cars through my imaginary town. Now I was more interested in playing baseball and planned to ask Santa at my next opportunity to bring me a real first baseman's scoop. Already I had become something of a craftsman in the sport in our neighborhood. Mine were some of the best homemade baseballs on our street, almost perfectly round with cotton twine from the mill looped around a small rock again and again until it had created a ball about the size of the real thing. There was a premium on roundness because Troy Sudduth, a left-hander, could transform the least imperfection into an unhittable curve ball. The trick was to select the perfect pebble as the starting point and then, after all the twine had been looped again and again until the ball was the perfect size, to carefully, tightly wrap the ball with black electrical tape. The final step was to roll the newly taped ball in dirt – the red clay dust beneath our house was perfect – until the tape that formed the cover of the ball was no longer tacky.

But good dirt could be found almost anywhere and bricking up my imaginary village beneath the house, and leaving it to spiders and such no longer was important to me.

"Just don't get in the way," the man had said as

he raked the hoe with the holes in it through the mortar one last time.

And I watched as he and several other men dug long channels beneath the outside walls of our house, poured long rows of fresh mortar there and, once it dried, began laying bricks row upon row until the bricks met the bottom of our house. Until this project had been started in our neighborhood, all the houses at Easley Mill, and most of the other mills in the South, had been built on brick pillars with the area between the floor and the ground left open so that when the winds of winter swept through the western end of South Carolina, we felt it first in the chilled floors of winter mornings.

Now that was going to change. Underpinning, they called it. I had heard that there was a mill village in Greenwood where the houses were all brick, and I wondered what it would be like to live in a brick house. But this, this underpinning, was as close as we would come.

The man stabbed his trowel into the stiff mortar again and again, leaving precise heaps of cement along rows of brick and mortar so that when he put in place new rows of bricks, the spacing was perfect, it seemed to me. His trowel flew again and again through the same routine, brick after brick. There was a certain rhythm to his work drummed out in the sound of gritty scraping and tapping.

In a sense, it was a thing of poetry. For his work and the work of an entire crew busy at other houses along our street profoundly changed the look and, indeed, the feel of our neighborhood. Houses built on a hillside not far away no longer seemed to be perched on gangly stilts, but now seemed to belong more gracefully with the flow of the land as did all the houses in the neighborhood. They seemed somehow more substantial.

"What ya going to be when you grow up?" the man asked, as he did his magic with mortar and brick.

"Maybe I'll learn to do what you're doing. What do you call what you do?"

"I'm a brick mason. Tough work, son. Take a look at my hands. Tough work. But the pay's good and I'm not cooped up in the mill all the time. Like the outdoors myself."

"Me too," I said. "If I decide not to be a brick mason, maybe I'll be a ball player, like my Uncle Wallace."

"Your uncle plays ball?"

"Yessir. First baseman at Glenwood Mill. Best first baseman I ever saw. Bet he could play professional baseball if he wanted to, but he doesn't want to." Just talking about baseball made me realize I already was making a career decision. I wasn't going to be a brick mason, no matter how remarkable seemed the work the man was performing beneath our house.

"You ever been to Ebbets Field?" I asked the man.

"What's an Ebbets Field? Know something about cotton fields, but that's about it."

"It's where the Dodgers play. Their first base-man is Gil Hodges. My Uncle Wallace is almost as good as Gil Hodges. Maybe better."

"Why do they call them the Dodgers?" he asked.

"'Cause they're good at dodging tags, I guess. Hard to get the Dodgers out."

"You think that's it?" he asked, uncertainty in his voice.

"I think so. But my Uncle Wallace would know."

The brick mason went his way, moving on to another house, and then another, until the entire neighborhood looked different, new again. And with special memories being the unreliable dreams they are, my Uncle Wallace still is the best first baseman I ever saw and I chose a profession not of mortar and brick, though I remember the man with the magic trowel when I return to that home on Third Street.

Though I have been gone from that house for more than 35 years now, returning only for brief visits, it still feels like home. And there still are times when I awaken in the dark of night and far away and for an instant imagine I am still there in the bedroom I shared with my two sisters beneath the big oak tree. It was the home of our parents for almost 50 years, and it is the place to which we, their three children each of whom now has children of their own and now grandchildren, return from time to time.

Perhaps it was the underpinning that con-firmed our roots there, the manner in which that mill company project made us feel more pride in where we lived, more settled. It is a house that seems today every bit as substantial as it did half a century ago, and it since has taken on a wing – a brick wing – that houses a modern kitchen and den with fireplace. My parents lived once again in a six-room house.

They were two gentle people who bought their first post-World War II automobile, a 1940 Plymouth four-door sedan, in 1949. Then in 1952 they bought on easy terms the house where we grew up when the manufacturing company, joining an industry-wide movement across the South, sold its houses, offering them first to the people who were living in them at the time, then putting them on the open market.

The Youngs, our neighbors across the street who were without children but who built a gold fish pond that fascinated us – it froze in the winter, its fish entombed in the ice until, we were told, they thawed again without mortal damage – left the mill hill with the first rumors that the houses would be sold. They built their dream home – of bricks – in Anderson County. But most of our neighbors stayed, increasing their still modest rent payments only slightly in buying the first and only house most of them would ever own. Houses that didn't sell sat empty, the grass and shrubs growing long and scraggly, until they were purchased by some stranger in most cases and converted once again into rental units.

Long ago, the company had built the houses in a successful effort to attract its work force, mostly from the dirt farms of the South. But by the time we were well into the cold war of the 1950s, good times had set in and the work force was becoming more mobile. The company's reason for owning houses to rent to its workers no longer existed.

My parents bought their home for $1,700 — "more than $3,000 if you include interest," my father once told me. It was a sum which would have seemed outlandish only a dozen years earlier when they moved two doors up the street from a six-room house that would become the new home of the Newsome family to the newer four-room house where the Boggs had lived until they found work at a mill in Greenville and moved away.

The move was economically beneficial to my parents as well because the rental price in those days was 25 cents a room per week, including water and lights. At $1 per week in rent, my mother and dad were saving 50 cents a week in an era when 50 cents was worth saving.

Fifty cents would have meant a lot to my grandmother at Glenwood Mill. She sold for a nickle apiece chilled Milky Way and Snickers candy bars that she kept in her ice box on the back porch of her mill house, and each profit of a dime she realized on each box of candy was put away in a special place until she had enough dimes to buy a round-trip bus ticket to Hartwell, Ga., via Anderson, to visit her relatives.

One of the negative aspects of living in company-owned housing was that there was a certain sameness about it, a sameness dictated by economic considerations. Mill company officials certainly understood the significance of the investment in housing and hired crews to maintain the buildings and occasionally contracted for improvements. The underpinning project was one such program.

The houses also were painted regularly by the mill's crews, who always painted the outside of the houses white. And just as often, they were there with paint and brushes to paint the insides of the houses, all the same color. At one such painting, the interiors of all the houses were painted a pale green, another time a subdued brown. Always the same, house after house.

All that changed, of course, when the houses were sold. Mostly maintenance-free asbestos siding in a variety of pastel colors began to appear on some of the newly sold houses, and so did Sears, Roebuck & Co. awnings. Our awning that shaded our front porch from the afternoon sun was a green and white combination and was among the first to appear in the neighborhood.

Being housing trend-setters was nothing new at our house where, long before the company's decision to sell, my parents invested in a standard of living that was special on the mill hill. Even though the mill crew also blessed the interior of our house with its company-issue green as it marched through the neighborhood on a painting binge, the uniformity was quickly shattered at our home. The uniform green soon was covered by my father with different, more pleasant hues in each of the four rooms, colors that were more to the tastes of our family so that when the insurance man knocked at the front door at our house and had it opened to him, he was aware that there was something different about the Browning home.

"Maybe you need some more insurance," he would say, perhaps uncertain what made this house seem unique.

The differences at our house extended beyond the color scheme. Long before the company made the decision to sell its real estate holdings, our family became only the second on the mill hill — other than the super, I would presume — to enjoy the luxury of a built-in bathtub.

I can remember Saturday night baths in the big galvanized tub placed back of the wood stove in the kitchen, and worrying about my modesty, but I remember only barely. Though we were too young to understand it at the time, our parents had made a commitment to an improved standard of living for their children, and for themselves, and when the war had ended, my parents ordered a fancy new tub from Sears, Roebuck & Co. With steel still in short supply because of the recent conflict, we had to wait for the delivery of the new bathroom fixture.

When it finally arrived and was installed in

our bathroom, company officials one by one called at our house and asked for permission to see the tub. Inspired by the interest, my parents then ordered matching bathroom fixtures including a new commode, an improvement that was especially significant for me. Unlike my grandmother's house at Glenwood Mill where two-hole outhouses still were being used and in which the only indoor plumbing was the kitchen sink, houses at Easley Mill had been built with indoor plumbing including flushing toilets.

But they were toilets which I, then in my late infancy, saw in my nightmares. They were equipped with wooden spring-loaded seats that opened when they weren't being held down by the weight of urgency. The urgency passed, the seats sprang open and triggered an automatic flushing action. It was an intimidating thing for a four-year-old such as I, with a bony butt and without sufficient weight to hold the seat firmly in place so that dismounting from the contraption seemed frightfully dangerous. More than once, as my weight shifted away, the contraption came close to knocking me to the floor in its zeal to flush.

So, a modern toilet with a handle for flushing was a welcomed improvement in my life.

Progress marched through our house in rapid order as well in heating and, eventually, window air conditioning. And at some uncertain point, the big kitchen wood stove of my very earliest years gave way to an electric range on which my mother, for a time, regularly burned bread.

My earliest memories, though, are of awakening on cold winter mornings to the rattle of the grate in the coal heater in the living room where my father was preparing a fresh fire for the day to warm our home.

"Stay in bed until I get it going," he used to say to me, and I would pull the warm sheet and Mother's handmade quilt up beneath my chin and listen to the sounds of the day beginning. In our pajamas, my sister and I would later stand beside the coal heater warming one side of our skinny, young bodies and then the other while the smell of homemade biscuits baking in the kitchen warmed our taste buds.

The leap progress next took was substantial, from the noisy coal heater to a Warm Morning oil heater that was quieter, cleaner and kept our house warm through the cold winter nights without having to be refired in the early morning hours.

We then became among the first mill hill families to install a built-in furnace and among the first to know the joy of air conditioning in the summer which, my father had said, was a necessity since he had difficulty sleeping in the steamy summer nights on the mill hill.

What we cannot claim to have been among the neighborhood leaders in was telecommunications. For most of the years in which I was growing up in the house at the end of Third Street, the only telephone in our neighborhood was the one in A.C. Walker's house at the corner of Third Street and Seventh Avenue. And the Walkers shared their phone willingly for special needs, such as phoning the doctor – who still made house calls in those days of few automobiles and fewer telephones – or taking calls from soldier relatives. And on those few occasions when we took advantage of the Walkers' generosity, we were careful to leave a dime or quarter there beside the phone, our way of telling the friendly family how much we appreciated their keeping us in touch with the world.

And one of the grandest of all moments at our own house was the day the growing phone company came to install our new instrument and assign to us our first telephone number, four simple digits we all still remember – 6066.

There also are few thrills to match the arrival of the first phone book, and turning to the "B's" and finding there confirmation that we were in touch with the world:

Browning, W.L., 712 S.3rd St............6066

Salvation
and the Midnight Train

I remember Garnet Owens being large for his
age, a teenager with big hands and a stout build,
an easy smile, a friendly manner, a round face
topped by reddish hair and freckles to match, and
a quick mind. Most people in my hometown are
related in one way or another to the Owenses, but
Garnet was not one of that set of Owenses and
that, by itself, set Garnet apart.

He and his family were outsiders. They had
come from somewhere else, transferring early in
the school year, with Garnet quickly becoming a
starting lineman on the high school football team.
An Owens who wasn't related to Red or J.B. or Pug
or Ben or Ray or Marion, who also was a starting
lineman on the football team, indeed was a curiosity in our neighborhood.

Garnet is memorable because of that and his
friendly nature. He is more memorable because he
is the first Catholic most of us ever saw. Finding
out that Garnet was growing up as part of a

practicing Catholic family was a shocking thing in our town, not something easily brushed aside. The day that bombshell hit, Garnet and his family became the subject of conversations at supper tables all over the mill hill. On the shock scale, it would have ranked right up there with stores opening for business on Sunday which, of course, certainly did not happen in our town. Except for drug stores where the pharmacist would show up on an emergency basis to fill a prescription, but don't ask him if he'd sell a pack of Wrigley's Juicy Fruit while you were there.

"It's Sunday," he'd say.

For a time, the Catholic thing affected the way we talked to Garnet and the questions we asked and the stock we put in his answers – though Garnet never seemed particularly concerned about all that. We knew we had to be careful, though, because we had been told again and again in Sunday morning and Sunday night and Wednesday evening sermons that situations just such as this were likely to come along in our lives to test our faith and that some of us might wander away, even to Catholicism. Still, there was youthful curiosity to deal with and Garnet just kept smiling and laughing and answering our questions while we decided if we were going to accept him even if he was Catholic.

After a while, we discovered that didn't much matter in Garnet's case, though we were sure he was very much an exception and that Catholics in general were not to be trusted, and liking Garnet became easy.

But from the beginning he had brought something new and strange to our lives, a fact that he seemed to understand and for which he was better prepared than were we.

He must have been warned that his family was moving into a neighborhood where the preachers were prone to be tough on Catholicism, where mixed marriages were those between Baptists and Methodists. For a lot of years, we had had enough religious differences to occupy our thoughts without having to deal with a Catholic in our midst.

But the folks at my church already had gotten a glimpse of what Catholicism must be like. The summer before Garnet and his family moved into the house on Liberty Drive, our church had held a revival that attracted a lot of attention. The visiting evangelist was the Reverend Grazzano, a man who once had been Catholic himself, who indeed had thought about studying for the priesthood, but who had experienced a remarkable conversion to fundamentalist Protestantism just in time. And he would tell us all about his former religion and it wasn't going to be a pretty picture.

So we had been warned beforehand so that we would later see the hand of God in all this. It was as though God had sent Reverend Grazzano, the former Catholic and almost a priest, to warn us of Garnet, and Garnet even confirmed much of what the evangelist had told us.

"You Catholics really eat fish on Fridays?" I asked him.

"Most of the time," Garnet answered, smiling.

"And when you Catholics pray, you pray to Jesus' mother, Mary? And not to God or Jesus?"

"Sort of," he said.

"Whattaya mean, sort of? Do you or don't you pray to Mary?" I had learned long ago that there was a certain danger in being soft with Catholics and communists.

"Well, okay. We do, but we believe that the Virgin Mary takes our prayers to God for us."

"Seems like a round-about route to me. They let us go direct," I said, feeling superior.

"I know," he said with a softness that hinted at deep wisdom, wisdom beyond his years and that knocked my superiority down a notch or two.

"And when you do something wrong, like cheating on a test, all you've gotta do is go sit in a little room and tell a preacher what you did and everything's all right, huh?"

"A priest, not a preacher. Yeah. We call it going to confession," he said, not trying to hide this theological flaw about which Reverend Grazzano had preached an entire sermon.

"Looks to me like you Catholics can do about anything and get away with it."

"Not really," he said, seeming to enjoy the whole exchange.

Garnet seemed comfortable with his religion and, though Reverend Grazzano had warned us that our minds could be stolen away without our knowing it, Garnet never tried his hand at converting us.

After a while, it no longer seemed to matter what Garnet thought about his religion, or ours. We had our hands full enough with the differences in Protestants.

Nothing exposed those differences like the street dances somebody at city hall proposed. The Church of God, Wesleyans and Pentecostals were solidly against it, the Baptists kept quiet and the Methodists and Presbyterians were in favor. Our preacher had predicted as much from the Methodists, in particular, and for a time Methodists and Presbyterians and how they had missed some important points of scripture became the hot topics for sermons.

The Methodists and Presbyterians won on the issue of whether there would be street dances, and for a time a portion of Pendleton Street downtown was roped off for orgies of sin, men dancing with women, actually touching, occasionally listening to jazz and only the Lord knew what else. And for a lot of the fundamentalists among us, the development represented a major crisis. More than one preacher found a parallel between Easley and Sodom and Gomorrah and predicted an end to life as we knew it in our hometown.

Even before the threat of Catholicism arrived in our town, most of us attended the churches of our choices with some degree of regularity. Only later in life would some of us come to understand that "old-time religion" had been more alive in our youth than we had appreciated at the time.

Could be that my own mother and father, without understanding the significance, were at the cutting edge of change simply by sitting together in their regular attendance at God's house. Perhaps without associating the practice with the ancient church, men and women, especially the elders of the church, sat on opposite sides of the aisle. Mother and dad sat together, always on the same pew, four rows back on the left side of the church.

Always in the same spot. Brother and Sister Porter, among others, represented the old ways, always sitting in the same – separate – pews preaching after preaching, just the way the ancient saints of Protestantism had done a century earlier.

It was at the back of the church where the teenagers sat, sweethearts holding hands, talking softly until an elder turned to stare them into silence or until the preacher moved away from the pulpit in mid-sermon and continued to deliver the message as he walked down the aisles of the church, so that his path took him uncomfortably close to the pews at the back of the church where the teenagers and young adults sat.

If anything, religion was a tight fit for a lot of us, especially at the church in which I was raised, a church that taught that a true believer should stand out in a crowd – "Ye shall know a tree by its fruit" – so that flashy jewelry, and short hair and makeup for women was frowned upon.

There were restrictions that went beyond appearances and included prohibitions against public swimming, for example, and participation in organized sports which is the one that wound up causing me most of the difficulty I had in walking our version of the straight and narrow.

Ours was mostly a fire-and-brimstone world, fraught with perils. Still, there was something special about being in church where Junior Cape played gospel piano with a talent and flair unique even in fundamentalist churches of which I was aware. And the singing always was inspirational with the Roach Trio and the Cape Trio always ready to answer a call from the pulpit for something special.

The price we paid for the music was the sermons, terrifying accounts of the after-death fate that awaited sinners everywhere, sermons that always ended with altar calls that, once answered, could last well into the evening.

Especially frightening was the night Brother Gilbert arose as the preacher sought to persuade lost souls to come to the altar. Brother Gilbert's growing family included two children only a few months younger than I.

"The Lord is coming back," he called out.

"Amen!" someone shouted.

"The Bible says that no man knows the day nor

the hour when the Savior will return," Brother Gilbert told the hushed crowd. "But I can say to you that here are my two children. I never expect to see them grow up before we all are called home."

"Amen!" someone else shouted, more loudly than the first.

"Won't you come," the preacher pleaded. "We'll wait for you and while we wait, shall we sing 'When the Roll is Called Up Yonder'?" And Junior Cape began playing slowly, softly while we found the place in our hymnals.

And then we sang.

When the trumpet of the Lord shall sound,
And time shall be no more,
And the morning breaks eternal bright and fair.

When the chosen ones have gathered
Over on the other shore,
And the roll is called up yonder, I'll be there.
When the roll. . .is called up yonder. . .
When the roll. . .is called up yonder. . .
When the roll. . .is called up yonder,
When the roll is called up yonder, I'll be there."

Now the preacher talked, pleaded, while Junior Cape played softly through another stanza and one by one sinners began to make their way to the altar.

It was a powerful moment in my spiritual life. So young, so unlikely, if Brother Gilbert was to be believed, to make it to adulthood, to big league baseball, before the world is destroyed, before we all heard the "trumpet of the Lord" and dead folks began to arise, followed by the good folks still living.

To me, it was a frightening possibility, not being one of the chosen ones when the trumpet sounded the end of time. So much so that late into the night, night after night, when the Atlanta-bound streamliner train out of Washington approached the downtown crossing and sounded its horn, I bolted upright in my bed terrified, certain that in the middle of the night I had heard the sound of the trumpet, not sure I would be going, frightened by the thought that I would be the only one in my family left to face the dreadful times.

Though I was never tempted to convert to Catholicism, there were times I wondered if Garnet Owens slept more soundly than I when the streamliner train whistled past the Easley crossing in the middle of the night.

The Galloways: Alvoid Galloway with daughters Imogene, left, Geraldine, on lap, and Beulah Jane, right, around 1948.

Quarantine

It came at the cruelest of times, the most fortunate of times, in the summer when school was out, at a time to be outdoors, in crowds, making new friends, spatting with old ones.

And the polio epidemics took all that from us, locking us into summer-long quarantine. Mill hill kids weren't alone in enduring the dreadful summers of fear. The polio scare ignored neighborhood boundaries, paid no attention to class distinctions, terrorized wealthy and poor alike. But we felt it deeply on the mill hill, though most of us were spared.

But not all of the people we knew.

Since she died in an early summer of the 1950s, so much has changed about Easley. Carolyn Tripp lived in a two-story house atop a hill where U.S. highway 123, once a by-pass that skirted our town, now runs, so that from the distance of these years it is difficult to find the patch of land that was the yard in which she once played.

Carolyn Tripp was not a mill hill girl, but many of us growing up in company houses listening to adults talk about how their "sides" had run that day knew her smile, her dark eyes and her coal-black hair. Though young enough to believe we would live forever, we thought of our own mortality the day word came that Carolyn was sick.

Polio, they said.

Polio always came in the heat of summer, when school was out, and we were lucky in that, though there were late summers when the opening of the fall sessions were delayed until close to first frost. There was something about the warmth of a southern summer that seemed to make weeds and polio grow rapidly. We came to understand that the crippling, deadly disease would be there in July and August and early September as certainly as violent thunderstorms which also frightened us, though their visits were more brief.

We were lucky though, because summer storms always seemed more violent than they really were in the summers when we were young, and all of the children who grew up on our street survived into adulthood on legs left untouched by polio.

We understood our good fortune, because polio would claim among its victims children like us at Alice Mill and at Glenwood Mill.

And it would devastate the Tripp family. Carolyn was learning to play the clarinet and had just joined the high school band as an eighth-grader in the spring before the summer when she felt an aching and then a numbness in her leg, a shortness in her breath.

And when school opened again in the autumn, Carolyn was not there. She was spending her late summer locked into an iron lung that pumped life into her thin body. The Tripps, we were told, had made room for the grotesque wheezing, pumping machine in the living room of their home where U.S. 123 now runs.

Strange that it would be the living room, because Carolyn did not live. She died, one of few people in our town to lose the battle with the frightening child-killer also known as Infantile Paralysis. And when she died, it was indeed as though we had lost a neighbor.

And when it happened, our own exile from our summers of freedom seemed a small price to pay. Church. It would be all right to go to church because there people would pray for healing and there, if we believed, we would be spared. But the gymnasium in the big building near the mill where company stores had served the community was pad-locked indefinitely and a swimming pool where mill hill folks once paddled through lazy summers was closed down and finally filled in. No one knew how long this killer, polio, would walk among us or how many generations it would threaten.

They still played baseball at Underwood Field, but to an adults only audience because polio seemed to be the province only of the young. And, I am told, even the baseball games were no longer the same, as though life also had been stolen from the men of summer as well.

And it could be that the threat of polio made of us all a generation of paranoid people. Mere growing pains, those twinges of discomfort in our legs and arms, took on potentially more frightening meaning, so that we learned to recognize even mild aches and to identify them as the first signs perhaps of polio. In those days, to have a toothache or an earache was considered a blessing.

Then, in the same summer in which Carolyn Tripp died, a few of us living near the end of Third Street learned that a sore throat could be life-threatening as well.

Beulah Jane Galloway and I shared the same birthdate, though I was a year older. Beulah Jane was the oldest daughter of Ina and Alvoid Galloway, who lived in the four-room house next door. Through much of a long summer, there was a fear that Beulah Jane would not live to get much older.

Diphtheria, and not polio, came that summer to the Galloway house and infected several of the children, Beulah Jane the most seriously. And when the highly contagious disease was diagnosed, health officials posted a quarantine sign on the Galloway's front porch there where the 25-50-75-100 order-card for ice by the pound once had been displayed.

"Beulah Jane is very sick," my mother told me the day the quarantine was posted.

"Polio?" I asked, expecting the dreadful answer.

"No. She has diphtheria. But she may die from

diphtheria just as quickly as people die from polio."

For a time, I thought I would prefer to be the
victim of polio. There were regular accounts in the
Greenville News of the number of children who had
been diagnosed as having polio, and there always
were the grim statistics of how many had died. It
was, however, obvious that some survived, though
their arms and legs may never again be the same
once the disease had robbed them of their elastic-
ity, their straightness, their coordination.

But from my mother's description of what
Beulah Jane was going through, diphtheria seemed
especially dreadful. "It causes a swelling in the
glands around her neck," my mother said. "She
may get to the point that she can't breathe and
then she would die."

The quarantine remained posted at the Galloway's door for three weeks, and Beulah Jane did
not die though for a time she was at death's door
unable to speak and almost unable to eat and
drink.

Indeed, we all survived the diphtheria and
polio scares and by the time we could resume our
summers in a normal fashion, so much had
changed. Including us. Earlier than most, our
generation had learned about mortality.

The author today, with grandson Caleb
Browning. Baseball still runs in this
mill hill-bred family.

Games of Summer

It was the summer of 1983, a long time and a lot of miles from the mid-century mill hill. My wife and I sat in folding lawn chairs back of the screen behind home plate at a Little League baseball game in which our youngest son was a participant.

Our son, Andy, seemed a grand figure to me in his uniform, the one with the blue shirt, white letters across the chest, my old high school number on his back, gray pants with a stripe down each leg perfectly matching the color of his shirt, stirrups of blue as well, and a blue cap. Beneath it all was a long-sleeved red warm-up shirt, just like that of all the other members of the team.

So different from the uniform my own mill hill team had worn that Saturday so long ago — almost 40 years ago. We had put together a rag-tag team of neighborhood kids and had issued a challenge to some of our friends on the backside of the village. The first game was to be played on our home field, the one in the pasture near my house, at 9 o'clock Saturday morning.

It was going to be a special game. Troy and

Marvin Sudduth, brothers from Fourth Street, and I had spent most of the week practicing in preparation for the big game. Troy, a left-hander, which was unusual on the mill hill in those days, would pitch for us. Marvin would play first base, the position I coveted, because he owned the best baseballs on our side of the mill hill. Marvin's baseballs were the real things, with unbroken seams and only mildly smudged by the red clay dirt of our infield. And that's how pecking orders were established on the playgrounds of our youth. I understood that code and I would settle for shortstop. And we spent most of the week trying to line up eligible talent for the remaining six positions.

There had been some ground rules agreed upon, among them that no one over 13 years of age would be eligible for either team. We had pushed for 13 instead of the 12-year limit the backsiders had wanted because the best hitter in our part of the neighborhood, Pokey Searcy, was already 13.

Determining which team would wear home uniforms was never considered because there were no uniforms, except those our team chose for the day. We agreed that each of us would wear short-sleeved shirts over pull-over sweaters. All the players on the Easley Mill team wore blue knit shirts beneath their uniform shirts and we wanted to be as much like the players on that team as we could. Besides, Troy's and Marvin's uncle, Paul Rampey, was one of the best players on the mill team and they had an image to uphold.

The Rampey connection was an important one. It was through that relationship that some of the broken bats from the big mill team found their way to our dusty diamond. But my only pull-over sweater was a bulky one of pale blue made of wool and it scratched at my bare arms in the oppressive heat of that Saturday morning as Marvin, Troy and I arrived an hour early for the game that would determine bragging rights on our mill hill.

And we sat there, along the third base line, which we had decided would be the home side of the diamond, awaiting the arrival of the rest of our teammates, and the arrival of the players from the backside. No one ever came to join the three of us sitting there in the July heat, growing restless in our sweaters. Not even Pokey for whom the special age-limit rule had been negotiated.

Since our team out-numbered the other 3-0, we claimed a victory by forfeit, sparking a neighborhood argument that would be debated openly, loudly among the 18 of us who had originally agreed to participate, and the disagreement would not abate until the chill of winter. It was a controversy that has not to this day been successfully resolved.

I was lost in those memories that late spring day in 1983. And now, there was Andy, our youngest, dragging a metal bat to the plate. Metal bats don't crack so that they have to be carefully tacked together again and wrapped with black electrical tape to both form a grip and to protect tender hands from the heads of carpentry tacks. With the metal bat at his side, Andy was dressed in his perfectly fitting baseball uniform, looking so grand. He fell away from an inside pitch as though it had been nothing more than an annoying mosquito.

"Dig in, Andy!" I called out. "Let him know you're not afraid of him." Scraping with his spiked baseball shoes at the dusty ground in the batters' box, Andy dug in, took a couple of practice swings and awaited the next pitch, a fastball on the outside corner of the plate. Andy swung and the ping of the aluminum bat announced a single to right and Andy made the turn at first and returned to the bag.

The first base coach, the team's adult assistant manager, patted Andy on the fanny and held up one finger. "Heads up. One out," he said as a reminder, and Andy nodded.

A teammate, one of the team's best hitters who in a few summers would be playing professional baseball, was next to bat and his father called out, as he always did, a set of instructions about the fine point of batting.

"Right elbow up," he called out to his left-handed power hitter. "Feet not too far apart. Swing through the ball. . ."

"Shut up and let the kid hit!" another father called out in annoyance.

"I'll shut up when I'm ready," the hitting coach-father shot back.

"You're obnoxious," the other man challenged.

The game had stopped and two teams of perfectly uniformed kids wearing real uniforms, playing with real baseballs, wearing real spiked shoes, each wearing his own glove, all with batting gloves stuffed in their hip pockets the better to grip metal bats – boys so different in their apparent affluence than we had been so many years ago – watched the commotion back of the home plate screen as the two fathers hurled insults at each other, growing more and more angry as they did, until the distance between the two was becoming dangerously little.

Finally, several other fathers arose as one and stepped between the two angry men, pushing them away from each other until calm had been restored and the game had resumed, this time without the loud coaching from the stands.

"I wish we'd had uniforms like Andy's when I was growing up," I said to my wife as our son once again took a conservative lead from first. "But not metal bats. They're just not the same. And I wish Andy could have played on the mill hill in the 1940s and '50s. We used broken bats, home-made baseballs, borrowed gloves, but we had it better."

"Why?" she asked, surprisingly calm since she too had watched the scene that had interrupted our son's Little League game.

"No adults."

No adults. No metal bats, which had not yet been invented. A lot full of kids who knew something of wood grain and how to expertly repair a broken bat so that slivers of wood would not split anew in the fixing. No honest-to-goodness umpires, such as those working our son's games, mostly because we didn't need them; we made our own calls, which were not in all cases popular decisions. In those now-ancient games of the summers of our youth, our arguments and our fights were relatively benign confrontations in which adults became involved only if our disagreements resulted in physical harm, which almost never happened.

Our disagreements were settled the old-fashioned way – someone took his bat or his ball and went home. But they would return a day later, the slate wiped clean and forgotten, to play games of roll-to-the-bat if there were too few of us for a game of choose-up-sides.

I'm not certain the slate ever was wiped clean as far as the two fathers at my son's Little League game were concerned. Summertimes and children's arguments were more simple on the mill hills of mid-century.

Indeed, the only game in which parents became involved were games of marbles. The Dunns were especially skillful at the games of knucksies, toys, agates and steelies and participated only in games of keepsies, which, our parents warned us, was a form of gambling and was thus strictly prohibited in most Christian households on our street.

But mostly, we were left to entertain ourselves in our games of summer, even some potentially as dangerous as tackle football.

In the summer, each of us had his own baseball hero. Mine included a Who's Who of Brooklyn Dodgers. When the heat of summer broke, we turned with the season to football and I sought to copy the jump-pass style of Johnny Lujack of Notre Dame, not aware in those innocent days that Notre Dame was a Catholic school. I was more interested in the doctrine of the jump pass than the doctrine of religion and learned that coordination was the important facet of jump-passing that I never successfully mastered in the Lujack style. I could jump and I could throw the football, but I could seldom do both at the same time. But to whatever degree talent failed us, imagination compensated. And I kept jumping and passing through the games of autumn after autumn.

Ours were mostly two- and three-man football games of tackle played on a sliver of grass on which the ends of our house served as the goal lines and the bushes lining the side our our house on one side and the mimosa tree on the other formed the out-of-bounds lines.

Which was not a precise thing and whether Harold Medlin had stayed in-bounds or had been knocked just ever so slightly out caused one argument after the other.

Harold was a quiet sort who always left the arguing to others and who had no football hero whom he openly sought to emulate, though we called him Crazy Legs for a simple reason. He had crazy legs. He ran at a strange, loose gait that made it appear his legs were going in different directions and he was thus particularly difficult to tackle.

But Harold had another characteristic that intrigued all of us. He didn't know how to cry. Ours were occasionally brutal games of tackle played without benefit of shoulder pads, hip pads, thigh pads, uniforms or helmets. And when Harold went down on a particularly hard tackle, we expected him to cry.

Instead, he giggled.

We discovered that the harder we hit Harold, the more it seemed likely to hurt, the more he giggled. He never said anything, never vowed to get even, merely giggled and limped back into formation ready for the next play, the next hit.

Unlike most of the rest of us, Harold remained near the mill hill of his youth and is today a quiet, smiling, graying man who operates a successful automobile tire business near Liberty Drive not far from the scene of our games of football nearly a half century ago.

Harold dropped out of our circle of young athletes about the time mill officials began to take a special interest in the activities of children growing up in the shadow of the big cloth plant. The building once used as a cotton warehouse just beyond the end of Fourth Street near the mill had apparently stood empty for several years when mill officials decided to renovate the structure as the home of a new village YMCA. Wooden floors, buffed and shined, were installed as were basketball goals. Two rows of bleachers lined each long wall and a small wire-cage office was installed at the distant end from where our new director of the mill YMCA would direct us.

The first of the few ever to move into that office was J.B. Owens, who had been an assistant coach at Easley High for a time. Though he was on the heavy side, he was the first first baseman I ever saw who could turn the stretch for the throw into the splits. He also had played college football and once was part of a military team that played against the old Brooklyn Dodgers professional team.

J.B. Owens was a man with a toothy smile who enjoyed sports, even those played at our elementary level. And he became the coach of the first midget football team organized on the mill hill, which was a considerable change from those backyard games in which we had participated, in that J.B.'s team had uniforms, hand-me-downs from the high school team, all of them too large so that keeping shoulder pads in place became more of a priority than blocking and tackling.

J.B. saw my own potential right away and assigned me to play right end, which is like sending the weakest player on a baseball team to right field against an all right-hand hitting team. And he taught me some of the fundamentals of the game, among them that good ends always play the wide part of the field and that good ones on defense force ball carriers to the inside where there should always be defensive help.

They were tough lessons practiced on a tough field near the mill where the community swimming pool once had been located before it was filled in, mostly with gravel.

And once winter had come on, he took us inside to the gym that once had been a cotton warehouse, and there he taught us the fine points of basketball - two-handed set shots, hook shots and bounce passes.

For the youngest among us, he secured a camping site and a dozen of us piled into his new Buick for the drive to a spot along a creek bank, which we spent the day clearing as a fitting place for our tents and camp fires. I made the trip in the front seat beside J.B. Owens, with my face not three inches from the radio which was tuned to a station playing "I'm Looking Over a Four-Leaf Clover."

Now, every time I climb into the passenger seat of a Buick even now, I have to resist the urge to break into song: "*I'm looking over, a four-leaf clover. . .that I overlooked before. First comes the sunshine and then comes the rain. . .*"

Dad, 1915-1990

So, we come to the final chapter of these recollections of the way life was on the mill hill, at least in the memory of one who was there and for whom these times and places and people have remained special.

It's late summer in the year 1990, and the early months of this decade have not been kind to the place and the people of my memories. The mill ran its final shift and shut down for good in January.

Imogene Galloway, the pretty little girl I remember from next door, whose older sister survived diphtheria and a long quarantine, died in the cold of last winter as she drove away from her first-shift job at one of the cotton mills yet running, her car crashing down a long hill and into those waiting their turn at a traffic light. She never knew it. Heart attack.

And a heart attack last spring took the life of one of the kids with whom I grew up. Hadn't seen him in so long he still was a tow-headed youngster in my memory, the oldest child in a family of two sons and two daughters. But when the obituary

At left, the author's parents, Martha and Willie Lee Browning, around 1947. This was Dad's favorite picture of him and his wife. Below, Martha and Willie Lee Browning in the late 1980s.

appeared in *The Easley Progress*, our hometown newspaper, my sister counted relatives. Only three sisters were listed. A miracle of surgery, we heard, had transformed the brother into another sister.

In June, workers came to cut down the old oak tree that had always shaded our house and the house next door where the Galloways and then the McCrickards had lived. The old tree had been there certainly when our house was added to those older ones along Third Street and it had been there as a strong, mature oak even when the first brick was laid in the building of the new mill in 1900. It had been witness to so much, to so many changes in the lives of our family, our neighborhood and our world, and like the rest of us, it, too, began to lose its proud erectness so that it tilted toward the very room in that special mill house where my two sisters and I nightly knelt to say our prayers. So comforting for so many years, the old tree finally became a threat and had to yield to the axman. But not to progress.

Our mother wept when the first power saws bit into the tree and asked if the three of us wanted chunks of the old friend for our own collection of memories. We did.

Then, on August 1, my father, who for so long had seemed as strong as an oak and as reliable, drove himself to the doctor's office and then to the emergency room at the hospital.

And died.

He had had a series of small strokes, had not

been able to drive for a while, but had regained his clear vision. We weren't ready for him to die.

We buried Dad beneath a young maple tree near the graves of his mother and father, two other lintheads we loved, in a cemetery filled with lintheads. He lies about as far from the grave of my buddy Harry Dalton as first base is from third.

Mother had requested that the Roach Trio sing at the funeral. "I'm sorry, Mrs. Browning," she was told softly, "but the Roach Trio almost never sings any more."

"They'll sing for him," she said confidently. And they sang like the angels. Calvin Roach, the tenor, was one of the pallbearers who bore my father to his place in the shade of the maple tree.

By autumn, Jack, my uncle and first hero, also was dead. He was buried almost within the shade of the maple that shadows my father's grave.

So, it has been a difficult winter, spring and summer along the streets of my youth. So much, it seems, was gone, missing from our lives.

For example, I had never fully understood the deafeningness of silence until I stood with Troy McCoy, long a friend of our family, on a pleasant summer day this year near the end of Fourth Street less than 100 yards from the old mill. Together, we listened to incredible silence of the stilled mill.

"Never knew it made a noise until now," the old weave room hand said.

But the mill didn't begin changing with the

coming of the '90s, or even with the '80s or '70s. We know now that it was changing even as we were living in harmony with the humming of spinning frames and the rattle of the weave room.

A lot of us marked the beginning of the end as the year they disbanded the old Easley Mill baseball team, and we blamed that on the blessing of television that came as one of the benefits of a postwar peace. But maybe the old textile league died for other reasons.

A historian who has studied such passings says it wasn't television at all, but air conditioning. When air conditioning units became portable enough to be fitted into the windows of mill houses, folks didn't wander out into the waning heat of summer evenings, to ball parks, neighbors' houses, to visit over back yard fences. They found their comfort in the humming of the air conditioning units in their windows. And that was that.

The major change could have been the sale of the company-owned houses and, indeed, that was an important point in the evolution of mill hill life. With that development came a self-sufficiency pleasing to the proud people of the mill hills, most of whom had never owned an automobile or a home of their own. By the late 1950s, most of them had both, and nothing ever again could be the same.

Those of us who were a part of the final generation raised in those company-owned homes might have seen the changes coming earlier in the decade had we been wise enough to understand that people, and communities, age and change and die. In our world, we were mostly concerned with sports, and in looking beyond the boundaries of mill villages for our futures.

Yet, we were at the tail-end of a string of generations in which it was generally conceded that there were but five major sports worth mastering – baseball, football, basketball, hunting and fishing.

Then George Owens began playing golf. A country club game. A game as foreign to people on the mill hill as soccer would be to those of us in the final generation. Had almost anyone else on the mill hill taken up this strange game, a trend perhaps would not have developed. But it was George Owens and that was important.

George was older than most of the members of the final generation to grow up on the mill hills, but not much. He was in the late 1940s a single wing running back at Easley High School, which had been built a long time ago within sight and within easy walking distance of Easley Mill. And he had played the game so well that as far as any of us were aware, he was the first person from our town chosen to play in the Shrine Bowl football game in Charlotte.

Stores in our neighborhood displayed in their windows pictures of Owens in his high school uniform, a football tucked under his left arm, with no helmet, with black, wavy hair combed neatly into place. Except for Paul Rampey and Juber

Hairston and the boys on the baseball team, he was the first great athlete to emerge from the mill hill. And that qualified him as someone who could, and did, set sports trends for us.

George had invitations to take his football talents on to college, but not many people on the mill hill had ever attended classes beyond high school and those who did went away to become bosses and supers in cotton mills. And George saw no reason for that since he intended – and succeeded – to operate the neighborhood gasoline station while the rest of us grew up and the old village continued its evolution.

And I learned only this year that George died, still young as those of us in the final generation view aging. He was not yet 60.

We were left with his legacy. If George Owens played golf, it was a game worthy of the efforts of a lot of the rest of us, and a handful of people at Easley Mill took up the game a long time ago.

We discovered as well that tennis could be a physically demanding game, and those of us who kept our distance from the country club golf course took up the court game and played it into the dark of summer evenings on the dusty dirt court that stood where a new wing of the old high school now stretches along Pendleton Street.

The beer joint on Fifth Street closed down, and except for the fragments of a brick wall cut into the red-earth bank, finally disappeared, apparently from lack of interest. Stores began selling six-packs and it was possible to drink at home, if one were so inclined. So the business that was no place for strangers closed its doors long before the cotton mill shut down for good.

Even our music changed. While some of us clung to, and still love, the big band era of our parents, ours was the generation that made room in our record racks for Elvis. Rock 'n' roll made it to the mill hills as the final wave of modern musical entertainment.

Ours was the generation that gathered along the Southern Railway tracks that ran through town to watch in silence the slow train that came through carrying the body of President Franklin D. Roosevelt, who had died in Warm Springs, Ga. When the train passed Glenwood Mill on its route north, an entire shift of workers gathered at the open windows of the old cotton manufacturing plant to watch and weep. He had been the only president a lot of us had known. He would not be the last, nor the last whose passing we would mourn, though the routes others would take to final resting places would never again pass through our town.

Finally, our generation was the one that changed its thinking most radically. For we were the first, in any significant numbers, to flee the spinning rooms and weave rooms of our parents and grandparents for other lifetime vocations.

Maybe that was the biggest change of all.